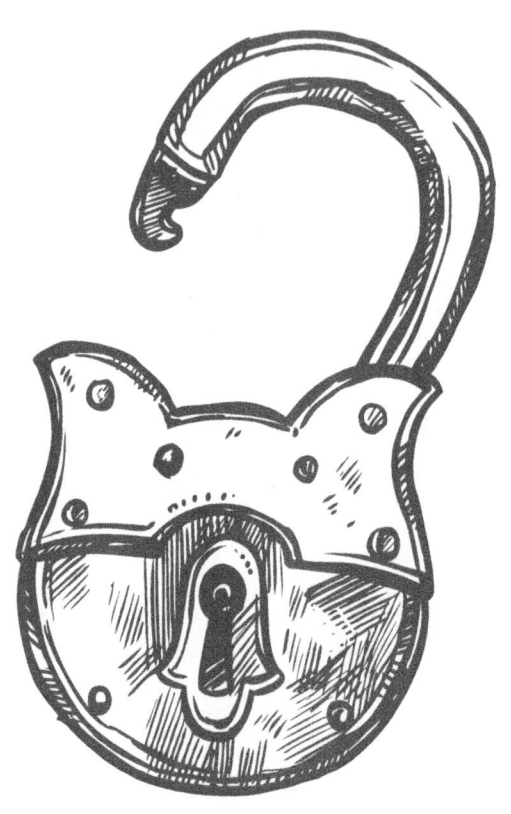

The Entrepreneur Escape Plan

"Working because you want to, not because you have to is financial freedom."
-Tony Robbins

"Being rich is having money; being wealthy is having time."
-Magaret Bonnano

"If your business depends on you, you don't have a business; you have a job. And it's the worst job in the world because you are working for a lunatic!"
-Michael Gerber

"Working hard for your business is good. Having a business that works hard for you and without you is much better!"
-David T. Fagan

THE ENTREPRENEUR ESCAPE PLAN

HOW TO OWN THE BUSINESS AND NOT THE OTHER WAY AROUND

JAS DARAR

The Entrepreneur Escape Plan: How to Own the
Business and Not the Other Way Around

Copyright © 2020 by Jas Darar, Founder
of REACH Business Coaching

www.theeeplan.com
www.reachbusinesscoaching.co.uk
admin@reachbusinesscoaching.co.uk

Published by Speaker House Publishing

Paperback ISBN: 978-1-7333441-6-6
Hardback ISBN:978-1-7333441-5-9

All rights reserved. No part of this book may be reproduced or transmitted in any form or by any means without written permission from the author.

Cover and back design by Michael de Hoyos Jr.
Edited by Vernon Fagan Jr.

Printed in the United Kingdom.

CONTENTS

Foreword — 1

My Father's Pain — 4

CHAPTER 1 — 9
The Cycle of Business Success

CHAPTER 2 — 13
Mastery

CHAPTER 3 — 14
Destination Mastery

CHAPTER 4 — 23
Mind Mastery

CHAPTER 5 — 50
Time Mastery

CHAPTER 6 — 71
Money Mastery

CHAPTER 7 — 87
Delivery Mastery

CHAPTER 8 — 91
Mastery Summary

CHAPTER 9 — 92
Growth

CHAPTER 10 — 106
Five Ways to Grow Your Business

CHAPTER 11 — 127
Growth Summary

CHAPTER 12   128
Leverage

CHAPTER 13   140
Leverage Summary

CHAPTER 14   141
Team

CHAPTER 15   196
Team Summary

CHAPTER 16   197
Freedom

Summary   *201*

ACKNOWLEDGMENTS

I express gratitude every day for all the blessings I have received in my life. I will also try and do that now for all the people who have helped me in my life:

Mum – you have not had a great life but thank you for protecting us from what my Father did.

Angela – there is not another person in the universe who would have put up with me like you have. Thank you for sticking by me through thick and thin; you deserve a medal. You are my best friend in the world and the best Mother I could have ever wished for for our girls. Thank you for being my girl.

Poppy and Jasmine – when you came along, everything changed. I just look at you, and I feel great. The words to express my love for you and my pride in you have not been invented yet!

Family – geography gets in the way, but I always feel safe and at ease when I am with any of you. Thank you for your love and support.

Friends – they say you do not need many friends, just a few good ones. I am lucky that I have a few good friends who I know I can trust with my life.

Clients – I learn so much from every single one of you every single day. Your strength under pressure and the breakthroughs you have are my inspiration. I could not ever wish to find more amazing people to help.

You – by reading this book, you are one of those special people who want to move forwards in life and want to take control and steer your ship. Thank you, you rock!

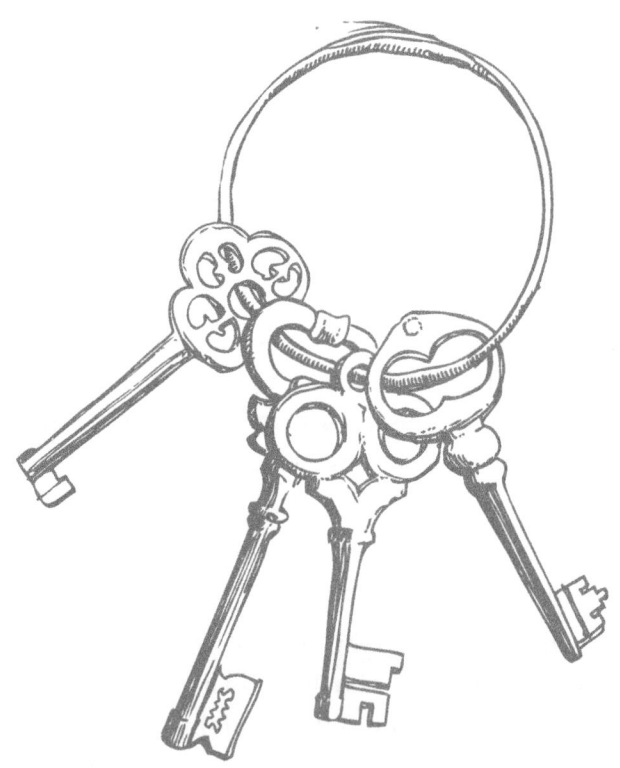

FOREWORD

You might have some bad news coming your way. You might even be in for what some would call a rude awakening. Answer me this: why did you get into business for yourself? Why did you start your own business in the first place?

Maybe you wanted to be your boss? Perhaps you wanted to work your hours? Perhaps you could not get the career you wanted, so you just created your own business to give yourself the job you always wanted?

You would not be alone if you answered yes to any one of these hypotheticals. So, how is that working out for you? Are you a good boss? What are the hours you work? Are you working longer than you thought? Are you feeling more like the owner of a highly profitable business, or do you have a suffocating job with lousy pay and very few benefits?

Again, you would not be alone. Very few people obtain the freedom they longed for when they first started their business.

Good news! It does not have to be this way. The author and business building expert, Jas Darar, knows how to raise a self-reliant, successful business. A successful self-sustaining business is what it means to have an Entrepreneur Escape Plan. It is all about building your business in a way that does not need you day and night. Your necessary participation 24/7 is a particular type of time slavery and a recipe for unhappiness!

Jas will get you asking the right questions and leading you to the best answers. You did not start a business for a job. You do not want to be a slave to your business, and you do not want to trade time for money.

You need systems, processes, people, and best business practices. You need to know where you are now, how you got there, and how to get out! This book teaches you how to do that.

Jas writes from his heart as the child of hard-working entrepreneurs that sacrificed too much. The family suffered and endured the endless cycles of the enslaved entrepreneur. Jas witnessed some things, both good and bad, that changed him forever. With his knowledge and wisdom, you do not have to suffer so much as you grow the right kind of business. Wow, he has some great stories!

You have a tough decision to make. You see, anyone can start a business and even run a business. The real question is, what kind of business do you want to run and own?

Do you want the type of business where you get to be the boss, seemingly in charge of everything? Is this what you want? Is that all you want? I dare you to want more. I challenge you to have an Entrepreneur

Foreword

Escape Plan. Jas will tell you how to become genuinely independently wealthy where your business works for you instead of the other way around.

Enjoy!

David T. Fagan

David T. Fagan is the former CEO of Guerrilla Marketing, which sold over 23 million books in 62 languages worldwide. David owned LCO Communications, a Beverly Hills PR firm representing 58 Academy Award Winners, 34 Grammy Winners, and 43 New York Times Best Sellers.

Fox & Friends, the Today Show, The Washington Post, Forbes, Investor's Business Daily, Your World with Neil Cavuto, The Five on Fox, and What's Happening has featured David. He has won major awards for publishing, publicity, and even the Entrepreneur Educator of the Year Award from Inc 500 Infusionsoft.

David is a best-selling author for several books, including *Word Genius: What to Say and How to Say It; Guerrilla Parenting: How to Raise an Entrepreneur; Cracking the Icon Code: How to Become an Icon in Your Industry Through Your Advice, Image, and Expertise;* and *From Invisible to Invincible: How to Make Your Presence Felt.*

He is an International Speaker in places as far away as Dubai, Bangladesh, Kenya, and Australia. He has shared the stage with everyone from former US Secretary of Defence, Dr. Bob Gates to Mark Victor Hansen.

MY FATHER'S PAIN

I have seen first-hand what happens when a business goes wrong. When I was younger, my father relocated us from my hometown of Derby in England, to Glasgow in Scotland. He ran a small newsagent shop on the outskirts of the city. He did what most business owners did. He did everything from cleaning the windows to going to the cash and carry. He stacked shelves, served customers, and sometimes even delivered the newspapers. At a certain point, things started to go wrong with this business. I do not know why. I was about seven years old at the time and had no idea.

The inevitable reaction from my father was to work more hours. Such was the pressure of this business. The business continued to fail, and my father worked more and more. It got to the point where my father and my mother worked over 18 hours per day. They tried to keep this failing business afloat and some food on our table. I cannot begin to imagine how this must have felt to my parents as the walls slowly began drawing in. Did they feel blind panic, shame, helplessness, and fear? Who knows, but it was not good.

After a while, my father started drinking heavily. The stress and responsibilities he felt during the inevitable collapse of his business led to his alcoholism. Further down the line, this alcoholism turned to violence

My Father's Pain

towards my mother. My three siblings and I were not on the receiving end of the violence. We had to witness the beatings my mother endured.

My mother put up with this for three decades and finally dared to divorce my father in the mid-'90s, no small feat for a Punjabi woman to undertake back then. My siblings and I ended our relationship with him then too. My father died about ten years later, with none of us having ever fixed our relationship, let alone spoken.

So, I can trace the entire breakdown of my family and the dysfunctionality that it has permanently left us with down to one thing. My father did not know what to do when his business began to struggle. Back then, business owners never had the plethora of knowledge and support people have now, especially at their fingertips. People certainly did not have access to Coaches and Consultants as they do now. The process of talking helps rationalise our thoughts. My father did not have a confidant. His ideas and then, of course, his actions became irrational.

So, why did you go into business? Was it some grand vision you had to change the world? Was it because you wanted more? Was it because you hated your boss? According to www.gov.uk, there were 5.9 million businesses at the start of 2019 in the UK. 5.9 million businesses was a net increase of 3.5% or approximately 200,000 businesses on the previous year. In 2018 about 595,000 businesses failed, or 1,630 businesses failures each day, and 2,180 businesses started each day. Either way, you did what people do every day around the world. You had what Michael Gerber calls an entrepreneurial seizure in his best-selling book, *"The E-Myth."* Whatever the reason, you did it; you leaped from safe, employed work to this crazy world where your boss now is a maniac! Better make it work then!

In this book, I hope to pass on to you all the knowledge that I have acquired running businesses and as a Business Coach. I have coached thousands of business owners since Jan 2007 and counting. I hope that in some way, this book will help you avoid business pitfalls, impacts on your health and wellbeing, and stress within your family. I will try and give you a step by step guide on what you need to do to start, build, and then grow a business that ultimately works without you. This book teaches you how to have a business and a life.

Before starting my coaching business, I spent a lot of time working for other people. I worked for some good people and worked for some not so good people. I worked and learned. At the age of 23, my cousin in Glasgow gave me a fabulous opportunity to run his bar-restaurant. As a new graduate with many debts, I was over the moon with this opportunity. I will always be grateful to my cousin for believing in me.

So, I jumped straight in with both feet at 23 years old. I managed the day to day operations of a large business with team members. I had zero experience, and I made a mistake after mistake. I cannot even list all of my mistakes. If I did, there would not be enough space in this book for anything else! When I look back on my life, though, I always seemed to learn the most and grow the most when I made the most mistakes. People are too afraid of making mistakes, so they do not rise to their full potential. They play it too safe. We are either growing or dying, so it is essential to keep moving forwards. If your business is a direct reflection of you, you must continue to grow and develop. So, my mantra is, *"making mistakes is fine!"* It is part of life's natural journey and should be welcomed and embraced, not feared. Please do not make the same mistakes time and time again though!

In mid-2006, my wife, Angela, was contemplating returning to work. She had been on maternity leave since late 2005. Our first daughter, Poppy, had arrived in early 2006. The birth of Poppy made me focus my mind on my responsibilities! One evening we were working out our finances, and I knew that we had a razor-thin budget. We had just purchased our new home, and of course, had a new baby too! While working in an excellent job as Operations Director for a large ISP, the numbers just did not add up. It was around then that an email landed in my inbox one morning. Thinking it was spam, I was about to delete it. Something compelled me to read it. It was from a franchise, and I liked what I read. I wanted to know more. After going through all the due diligence, I began my training and started my first business as a Business Coach in Jan 2007. I always knew I wanted to start my own business, and this was my chance with the help and guidance of a franchise.

I am a big believer in doing your first business

through some sort of support network. A franchise, online community, or another type of group can provide the necessary support. Support, guidance, and systems you get are invaluable. Indeed, recent research has shown that franchises offer a model with:

- A Proven Operational Concept with detailed "how-to manuals."
- Less Risk than a Start-Up.
- Market Demand for the Product or Service.
- Established Customers.
- Other Franchisees to support you.
- A launch process that is easier than with a Start-Up.
- Statistically more chance of success.
- According to www.investopedia.com, on average, 65% of start-ups fail, and on average, only 25% of franchisees fail.

The evidence is conclusive. With the right support, you have a greater chance of making your business a success. Indeed, I would not have been here today if not for the support I received, especially in those critical early days.

If you are going to start a franchise, please leave your ego outside! It is astonishing the number of franchisees that invest huge sums of money in a franchise and do not use the information they just paid for because they think they know better. Bonkers!!! Pay your money and soak up as much information as you can. I promise it will help you.

CHAPTER 1

THE CYCLE OF BUSINESS SUCCESS

I developed this model over the years. Many people around the world use the model daily. The model gives consistent results. The model is much easier to work, versus someone just freestyling their way through their business life. Freestyling works for some people, and I salute them, but it is not for me. I would rather have a system.

Here is the model.

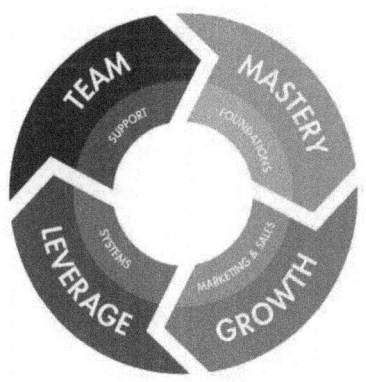

One significant change I have made from other similar models is that my model is a cycle. Too many other models denote the ladder, suggesting that you have got it sorted once you reach the top. Many business owners think that they will wake up one day, open the curtains, and a shaft of sunlight will rip through the room with a blast of *"Hallelujah"* music. If that happens to you, worry. You have died and are in heaven. By its very nature, a business will continue to throw challenges at us on a minute by minute basis. When the principle of *"Kaizen"* is embraced, it is about *"constant and never-ending improvement."* It does not stop. The only time it stops is when you sell, put an MD in, or close the business down.

Before I go into the different areas of the Cycle Of Business Success, I need to explain the overriding philosophy behind them and how they link together.

Mastery

Mastery is all about the fundamental building blocks of any business. Without these, it is like trying to build on sand. It will only take so much strain before it collapses. How long the business lasts is linked to how fast and long the business owner can keep running. I hope you will agree; this is not sustainable. We need something to hold this business up and keep it up. Mastery is broken into five key components:

1. **Destination** – Where are you going? What is the aim? What's your exit strategy?

2. **Mind** – How will you train your mind to serve you instead of being a slave to it?

3. **Time** – How will you become an expert in getting more done in less time?

The Cycle of Business Success

4. **Money** – What knowledge do you need to get to understand your numbers?

5. **Delivery** – How will you ensure that every customer interaction is the same?

Once you have Mastery, you know that you can start to grow this business. You can feel safe in the knowledge that it has an excellent chance of not only surviving but thriving, and giving you a business to be proud of and a life worth living.

Many people ask why they cannot do all the marketing and sales work, which is next in the model, first. Mastery is first for a reason. For example, usually different things sell for different amounts making different profits. You need to be clear on profits and losses on the things you sell. Without realising it, you could sell more loss-making items and bankrupt yourself quicker than you would anyway! You need to know what makes what levels of profit before you start marketing for new sales. Also, if you are already working 80 hours per week, you will not thank me for making you even busier! You need Mastery first; then you can grow.

Growth

Growth is where all the *"sexy"* marketing and sales happen. It is where you can start building the business. But remember, bigger does not always mean better. It is about profitable growth that helps you achieve your objectives. It is not about any customer with a cheque book and a heartbeat!

Leverage

For me, this is the real secret of making a business scale. I always want you to remember; systems run the business, people run the systems, you lead the people. As you undoubtedly grow, you do not want your costs to continue to rise proportionately. You want things to scale. You want profitability to increase even more. Systems let you do this and many other great things that you will learn about in this book.

Team

Here is where we look at how you manage, lead, recruit, train, keep, and remove people. One of the biggest frustrations and fears that business owners have is managing people. It is such an alien concept to so many that you may as well be talking Swahili to them! This inability to manage people stops business owners from growing their businesses, and it is a real shame because there is a better way to manage a team. I have always believed that the *"team"* can either make your life relatively easy or very hard.

Freedom

Now, you have systems running the business, people running the systems, you can employ someone to lead your people. You now have a particularly important word to human beings, choice. You can choose to go to work, or you do not have to. It is when you do not have that choice that you begin to resent the business. I am all about giving people the option to do whatever they want to do with their lives. After all, life is too short!

CHAPTER 2

MASTERY

Mastery is all about the basics. We need to understand these basics to make good, reliable decisions based on facts, not guesswork. Without Mastery, we will always be one step away from another disaster, living every day on the edge, not knowing if we will still have a business tomorrow.

Have you ever seen, or run yourself, a business that seems to grow a little and then always comes crashing down? Well that's because no foundations are holding that business up. In effect, the business is built on sand, which, eventually, will give way. Typically, the only thing holding the business up is the tired and weary business owner.

We need to lay these foundations to support the business now and in the future.

CHAPTER 3

DESTINATION MASTERY

What is your *"why?"* I ask everyone I ever work with to understand their *"why."* What is that thing that will get you out of bed every day, regardless of how many things go wrong and how many setbacks you have? And by the way, business owners have setbacks by the bucket load!! That *"why"* must be personal, not business-related. It must be like a burning flame deep in your heart. And when something goes wrong, the *"why"* will help you keep going until you get the desired result. One of my favourite phrases is that *"no one fails until they give up."* If you can clearly define your *"why"* you will not give up, and you will eventually achieve your goals. Get clear on your *"why"* and get to know the *"why"* of your teams. That will help you manage them and get better results out of them.

Have you ever heard the phrase *"be careful what you ask for because you just might get it?"* Well, this is true in all aspects of life, especially business. In your brain is the Reticular Activating System (RAS). The RAS is like a compass for your brain and makes the things that you ask for show up in front of you.

Have you ever wanted a dream car? What was it? When you got clarity on what car it was you wanted,

Destination Mastery

did you notice that cars like that started appearing on the road all the time? That is not magic; it is your RAS making the things you focus on, show up. On the flip side are the things you do not want to show up in your life. You see, the RAS does not know the difference between what you positively wish to show up in your life and what you are actively trying to avoid. It does not discriminate. Do you have that friend who says it always rains when they go on holiday? It probably only rained for one day of their 2-week holiday, but they set their RAS on a rainy holiday. The friend focused their RAS on rain, so the friend saw rain, and nothing else. Too many people focus on what they do not want, not what they do want. For example, if your only goal is to get out of your overdraft, guess what you set your RAS on finding? More overdraft. Instead of focusing on a negative, why not change the language to a positive instead? For example, the goal is not to get out of overdraft; it is instead to have a business account balance of £100k by the end of the year. Tell your RAS what you want and be clear about the language you use.

Before setting any business goals, you need to do something that most business owners do not do, put yourself first. There is a negative connotation associated with the word *"selfish."* People view this word as immoral, malicious, and greedy. For me, *"selfishness"* is a healthy state. When on an airplane, whose oxygen mask do they tell us to put on first in an emergency? Even if we have children, they tell us to put our mask on first. We cannot help anyone else if we are not okay first. How can we give more to our family and friends, our community, help more people in need, and create more jobs if we are not okay first? That is why putting yourself first is a necessary discipline to master, especially in goal setting.

The business should be the vehicle that you, the business owner, sits on, leading you to your life's objectives. It usually gives you fuel, or money to burn, allowing you to achieve what you want to accomplish before leaving this earth. So, hard as it may seem, you need to stop and ask yourself the question that you may feel uncomfortable asking. What do I want? What things do I want for me and my family? What experiences do I want? Where do I want to go? What feelings do I want to feel? Who do I want to help? How many languages do I want to speak? Answering these questions can be a tremendously exciting and liberating experience. For those going through tough times in their business, this can provide a real spark and re-energise them.

Think of yourself as a separate entity from the business. The diagram in Appendix 2 shows the business structure, pointing to the pinnacle at the pyramid's point, which is the business goals. Above that is the business owner being delivered their life's objectives by the business. You can access Appendix 2 at www.theeeplan.com.

Dream Chart

Your eyes are your most robust sense. Your eyes feed the part of the brain where the RAS is based, the subconscious. Whatever images your eyes see and focus on, your RAS will make more of that show-up. Remember, your RAS does not know the difference between what you want and what you do not want. So, it would make a whole lot of sense to feed your eyes with some good, healthy, and nourishing images of things you want in your life.

One task I ask all my clients to undertake is to create a Dream Chart. A Dream Chart is a selection of images of things that you want in your life. They could be materialistic, spiritual, travel, experiences, hobbies, or absolutely anything it is you want in your life. The manifestation of your Dream Chart is your choice. Some of my clients buy these gigantic picture frames and fill them with images they printout from the internet or magazines. Some like to create a printout from electronic images or buy a digital picture frame. Some have it as their screen saver on their computers. Some have it at work, and some have it at home. Whatever form it takes is up to you; there is no wrong or right. But it must be somewhere where you will see it daily, even if it is just in your peripheral vision. You do not have to stare at it and pray to it either!

For many businesspeople thinking of things they want for themselves can be extremely hard. After all, they have spent an enormous amount of time thinking of everyone else and usually taking what is left, if anything. As I have just mentioned, you must master putting yourself first, however hard it is. Thinking of yourself first takes time. Please stick with it and have some fun! Dare to dream. Get your loved ones involved in creating the Dream Chart. For those of you with young children, this can be an exciting process and adds to the pressure positively. If your child wants to put Disneyland on the Dream Chart, you had better make enough money to take them!

If you are not the most creative type, you might need some help finding things for your Dream Chart. We are blessed to live in the information age. We have all the resources known to humankind at our fingertips. Try searching for things like *"dream chart ideas," "vision board ideas,"* or *"bucket list ideas."* You will find more items than you ever dreamt possible with these searches alone.

The power of the Dream Chart and having it visible daily became clear to me many years ago. I had my Dream Chart on another desk in my office. Sometimes, weeks, if not months, would go by and I would not even sit at that other desk, let alone see my Dream Chart. One day during a Coaching session, a client of mine, Andy, who was involved in print and design, asked if he could take my Dream Chart away. Andy wanted to turn it into a nicely designed and branded JPEG for me. Then I could have it as a screen saver on my flat-screen TV. The same TV that I used in my Coaching room during every Coaching session. I agreed that this would be a great idea, and a few days later, Andy emailed me my Dream Chart as a JPEG, which I promptly turned into my TV screensaver.

Previously, my Dream Chart had been on my desk, and in two years, I achieved nothing from it. Within six months, with no extra conscious effort, I realised I had completed just under half of the things on my Dream Chart. I attribute the new level of completion to my TV screensaver in front of me daily and continuing to feed my RAS with *"good food."* I do not know how this fully works, but as Bob Proctor says in the film The Secret, *"I don't know how electricity works, but it doesn't stop me from using it!"* I know it works, and I continue using it. I, along with my girls, update our Dream Charts when we have achieved things off it. We know that the hard work we do in our businesses allows us to achieve our dreams. This phenomenon motivates and fulfils us.

From a coaching perspective, I connect with my clients through their Dream Charts more than anything else. It is like opening the door to their deepest desires. Their Dream Charts help me understand them at the deepest level possible!

I also ask my clients if they should know their team's Dream Charts. Can you imagine how many more *"buttons"* you could learn to press with your team if they all had their Dream Charts visible at work? Can you imagine the connection work colleagues would have with one another by seeing each other's Dream Charts?

12 Month Goals

It is vital to set your RAS on the things you want, not what you are trying to avoid, especially when it comes to an essential part of Destination Mastery - goal setting. Goal setting is about programming your *"Sat Nav"* with the correct GPS coordinates. Your *"Sat Nav"* ensures your arrival at the right destination safely and on time.

A study follows a university graduating year for 25 years. A different university is chosen every year. After 25 years, the graduates are revisited, and the study has found that only 3 % of the group wrote down their goals and had them visible. Yet, that same 3% accounted for 98% of the wealth of that graduating year, every year, for the 50 plus years this study has been going on. I hope you will agree; this cannot be a coincidence!

You should always have your 12-month goals visible to you daily to cross-reference your behaviours against. If what you are doing today is not leading to your goals, why are you doing it? Visible goals will also keep you focused through the year, so you do not just look at them on the 31st of Dec and think, *"Damn, it is too late to achieve them now!"* As a family, we have our 12-month goals too. One day in January, my eldest asked me if we could go out on a Dad and Daughter date. We do this anyway, but I was intrigued as to why she wanted to go right then. She replied that it was one of her 12-month goals to have a date with me every month. She did not want to fall behind on her target. She remembered her 12-month goals because she had them stuck up on her bedroom wall. We must keep reminding ourselves to take action daily to achieve our goals.

Goals also need to meet the SMART test. SMART is an acronym for Specific-Measurable-Achievable-Realistic-Timeframe. Too often, the tiny percentage of business owners who do have goals have made them so *"wishy-washy"* that they do not even know if they have achieved them. Never mind if they should crack open the bubbly to celebrate. That is because the goals were not SMART. Imagine two business partners. Imagine in their 12-month goals they said they wanted to make more money. Imagine that they earned £50k more profit, and partner one is doing high fives and cartwheels of joy at the end of the year. Imagine how conflicted partner two would be because he had wanted to make £100k more profit that year? In this instance, the goal was not SMART enough. So now you have a grey area. Ensure it is black or white, or if you have or have not achieved the goal at the end of any specific period. There cannot be any doubt. Make your goals SMART.

You must start with the end in mind and know your exit strategy. And even more importantly, when it will be. If you do not assign a deadline, it will never happen. Once you have defined your deadline, you need to work backward and set annual goals to achieve this end goal. Everything you do daily will now have purpose and meaning because it leads you to the end goal.

It is also vital that you share your goals with the team. Sharing your goals can prove to be scary for the vast majority of business owners. After all, *"what would the team say if they saw how much money you wanted to earn?"* My opinion is that if they have a problem with this, they should not be on your team. What I find is that most people are good people and want to help you achieve your objectives. If you share your goals, then their response may surprise you. With that focus, your people may start coming up with new ideas to help achieve your objectives in a way you had not considered. What is there to lose by sharing?

CHAPTER 4

MIND MASTERY

I have always believed that our mindset is our USP. It will be the difference between success and failure. We must protect it and nurture it by feeding it only healthy *"food."* We must be conscious of what goes into that grey matter upstairs! Far too many people think that mindset issues do not affect them. In my experience, mindset issues affect everyone. It is just that some people are more conscious of them than others. Being aware of what is going on *"upstairs"* is the first step to moving forwards because once we are aware, we can do something about it.

Self-Care

Too many business owners spend so much time thinking about everyone else's welfare that they neglect to look after themselves. This noble behaviour is flawed. As mentioned previously, when the airplane attendant does the flight safety demonstration before take-off, whose oxygen mask do they tell you to put on first? Yours, of course, because if you are not okay, how can you help anyone else? The same applies to your business. How can you help your customers, suppliers, team, community, or charities if you are not okay?

As mentioned previously, the word selfish has many negative connotations associated with it. But for me being in a state of selfishness is the best state you can be in so that you can help so many more people.

We can all remember times when we were on fire. We were *"smashing"* it every day. Then there are all the other times when we did not even have the energy to get out of bed, let alone drive a team and business forward. Capturing the winning formula is so important that I always ask my clients to list all the things they do when they are *"cooking on gas."* What are the ingredients you threw into the pan that created such a great result? If you do not write it down, you will miss one out one day as sure as night follows day. Then the next day, another will get forgotten, and before you know it, you are in a rut again. Write it down and create a self-care checklist to ensure you add the important things into your *"pan"* every day.

Imagine standing on a plinth that is held up by many vertical pillars. If there are many pillars, the plinth stays strong and does not wobble, even when there are strong crosswinds. These cross winds come every second of every day when running a business! Imagine taking some of the pillars out, especially from the edges of the plinth. Now it is more likely to mean we may wobble a little bit if we are not careful. Too often, most people only have one of two pillars and are much more likely to fall off the plinth when there is a gust of wind. The areas discussed next are the vital *"pillars"* of keeping you well looked after and stable:

- **Sleep.** Sleep is your secret weapon. Use it wisely. Protect and cherish it. Make sure you get enough of it. All sorts of research is out there, and conventional wisdom says 8 hours per night. The body and mind need time to renew and replenish their lost matter every day.
- **Diet.** Everyone is different, but if you listen to your body, you will know which foods make you feel good or make you feel slow and sluggish. All manner of tolerance testing kits can be purchased online to show you what foods you should avoid. Please remember, input = output. If you put petrol in a diesel car, it will not work. Fill your tank wisely.
- **Hydration.** For all my adult life, I have always drunk at least 3 litres of water a day. I have a water distiller. If you go down this route, please remember to add the essential minerals back into the water. I add Celtic Sea Salts to replenish the minerals removed during the distillation process.
- **Exercise.** Who does not feel amazing after exercise? When the endorphins are flowing through the blood, our mind is clear, and we can take on the world. As Robin Sharma in his book, "The Greatness Guide" says, "30 minutes of exercise a day will transform your life and your business." People vary on when to exercise. I prefer 30 minutes every morning.

- **Mindfulness/Meditation.** The research continues to stack up on the benefits of meditation and mindfulness. This process helps me experience the incredible sensations that gratitude creates in the mind and body.
- **Education.** Knowledge is all around us, and as one client once put it, "reading doesn't just give me knowledge, it also gives me the confidence to try things." Education nourishes the mind and gives it a reason to keep growing and developing.

I am not saying these pillars are right for everyone. Yet, in my experience, I have found that often these are the ones that make all the difference.

Belief Systems

Beliefs are things that we believe to be true. Beliefs can be changed, just like that. For example, some people's beliefs around religion can change with the passing of a loved one. In a business context, we must understand our beliefs, and if any of them are holding us back.

One belief system I see holding people back is that *"people can't be trusted."* Can you imagine if you had people working for you, and this was your belief? How would you ever let people do their jobs? How would you delegate to them so that you could get on with doing what I call the £500 per hour jobs? You would not! You would waste a lot of money on someone's wages for you to simply do their job for them. Or worse still,

Mind Mastery

micromanage them out of the door they came through! Usually, this lack of trust stems from a time where a business owner has been stung. They no doubt trusted someone, and that someone let them down. Instead of looking to see if systems and processes were to blame (they are 94% of the time), they decided that no one could ever do it as they do. And if a job's worth doing, you may as well do it yourself. Sound familiar? No wonder the business owner is now working 20 hours a day!

Another belief system I see often concerns money. Many people have deeply held beliefs about money, especially that *"money is the root of all evil."* If this is your belief about money, I am sure that you will be subconsciously sabotaging yourself. You will stop yourself from achieving what you want to. By the way, money is not everything. There are lots of things in life that are much more important than money. Yet, it is the universal language of business, so we do need to understand it.

Many years ago, I coached someone who was deeply religious. Their belief system was that *"money is the root of all evil."* This belief system would continue to sabotage them as we tried to grow the business. I needed a way to remove this block. I asked my client what he could do with an extra £50,000 in profit every year. Could he possibly donate some more money to his Church? Of course, he could. That one shift of the deeply ingrained belief system was enough to release the handbrake and get him moving forwards towards his goals. The resultant change was so significant that his biggest goal, to retire before he was 55, was achieved four years ahead of schedule!

Another time I came across a gentleman in his mid-50's. During our initial discussions to see if we could work together, he presented me with his last three years Profit & Loss statements. I noticed that net profit before tax was:

Year 1 - £49,300

Year 2 - £49,750

Year 3 - £49,400

Confused, I explained that I had never seen a business where the net profit had been so consistent. He replied, *"That is not a surprise to me. You see, when I was growing up, my Dad always told me that I would never make more than £50,000 a year."* When the last words of that sentence left his mouth, the colour drained from his face, and he realised what he had just said. Remember, this man was in his mid-50's. He adopted the limiting belief system taught to him by his father, and it influenced him for all his life!

You may have your foot firmly pressed down on the accelerator. The engine might be screeching, and there may be smoke coming out of the exhaust. The wheels may be spinning and burning rubber. Yet, if the handbrake is up, you are not going anywhere! So, what belief systems do you have that may be holding you back? Remember, being aware of something allows you to do something about it.

Values

Have you ever had a time where you just got on with someone you just met? People say, *"I had a connection with them"* or *"we just clicked."* This is because you had shared values. Values cannot be changed. You acquire a set of values by approximately seven years old. Values are the point of reference you use to make all your decisions, both conscious and subconscious. Defining these values and knitting them into the fabric of what you do daily in business is especially important.

Not every decision you make is going to be universally popular. Yet, when you go to sleep at night, your conscience must be clear. The only way you can do that is to have made your decisions using a set of values. That way, no matter how tough the call, you know you acted correctly and consistently because you used a value system to make that decision.

Imagine walking into your office, and one of your team had left a mess everywhere. You noticed a spilled cup of coffee, a half-eaten sandwich on the desk, and several screwed-up pieces of paper on the floor. Most bosses walking into this situation would not be happy. Typically, the boss initiates a conversation, usually starting with the words, *"What the bloody hell is this??!!"* This situation can become a conflict because it is one person's opinion of what is acceptable versus another person's opinion.

Now imagine a similar situation where the company values had been defined, agreed to by everyone, and visible on all the office walls. Imagine if the boss was confronted with the same scene, but in this instance, they simply asked, *"How does this fit with our value of excellence?"* Of course, this scenario assumes that *"excellence"* was one of this company's values. Now the individual concerned can hopefully respond in a less antagonistic manner. A better discussion can occur to come to a more meaningful conclusion and ensure that this situation did not happen again. When you do not have your values defined and visible, it is one person's opinion versus another. When you do, you ask people to adhere to the company standard, not one person's view. And remember, everyone in the team must sign up to these values, or they cannot stay on the team.

You can use values to deal with problem customers. You know who I mean! The customers who always:

- Haggle on price.
- Pay late.
- Complain all the time.
- Insist on talking to the "boss."
- Go out of their way to bad mouth you.
- Leave you or your team in tears.
- Make your life a misery.

Well, let me enlighten you! You do not need to work with them. Can you imagine sending them a letter or email listing your company values and asking them to stick to them from now on? Can you imagine telling them that they will have to find another business to use

Mind Mastery

if they do not? Defining and using your values is so helpful in so many ways! Until you *"sack"* one of these *"D"* grade clients, the universe will keep sending you more. (More on ABCD clients later).

Here is how I go about helping people define their values. Print out Appendix 3 and hand a copy of it to everyone in your business. You can access Appendix 3 at www.theeeplan.com.

Ask them to take it home and to pick their Top 20 values. The values that mean something to them. The ones that they want to live and breathe in their place of work daily. Give them a week to pick, and then call a team meeting to discuss them. After a good discussion, narrow the values down to 12. The best way would be to rate each value based on how many people had it in their Top 20. Yes, this discussion might take a while. You might need to reconvene again later; however, going through this process with the team means that they have a commitment to living these values because they helped define them.

Once you have a consensus on your values, make them visible inside the business. Try to use them and refer to them daily. Discuss them. Highlight examples when people have displayed behaviours that show they lived by the values. Get them embedded into what you do so that you not only talk the talk but walk the walk. By living the values, you will lose non-compliant team members. After about a year of making sure you adhere to the values, you can go public. Put them on your website, correspondence, and company cars. Put them everywhere! Please make sure you stick to them. It will make your life and your team's lives so much easier.

Some people ask me how to remember all the values daily. Having them visible would be an excellent way to start to remember them, but I appreciate that you will not always be in your place of work. That is when I rely on my gut instinct when processing situations and making decisions. Recent studies have found brain cells in the lining of the gut and the heart. This fact lends weight to the phrase, *"listen to your heart, or trust your gut."* Our gut instinct is a system designed to protect us. It is there for a reason, and I wish more people would listen to it and act upon it. If something does not feel right, then more than likely, it will not be aligned to your values. If it feels right, do it. Your decision will sit more comfortably with you because it was in alignment with your values. Over time, I have become better and better at listening to my gut. I can report that it has led me the right way most of the time so far.

Identity

When each of us is born, a tiny little imaginary parrot goes and sits on one of our shoulders. This parrot stays with you for the rest of your life. The imaginary parrot repeats in your ear 24 hours a day, seven days a week, the negative I AM statements you experience throughout your life. The parrot feeds on the constant negative things that are said to you, especially during your formative years. For example, the 8-year-old child told by their teacher that they would never be good at mathematics. The child will undoubtedly go through life repeating, *"I AM no good at mathematics."* These negative I AM statements are incredibly destructive and will hold you back if you let them. If behaviour follows identity, you must understand what you are saying to yourself because if you want to change your behaviour, you need to change your identity. This is because what you say to yourself about yourself when you are by yourself are the most important conversations you will ever have. Once you identify these negative I AM statements you speak to yourself, you can do something about them because these I AM statements contribute to self-criticism and affect your behaviours. Self-talk has the power to destroy or improve your life.

Years ago, a large company advertised for a senior management position in the national newspapers for one week. The role would pay the successful candidate £250,000 per year. Not bad work if you can find it! After a week, they had received one application. The following week they ran the same job advert in the same newspapers with the same job title and job description. But this time, they put the salary at £50,000. They received 37 applications that week! Think about the negative I AM statements that held people back in the first week.

My alcoholic and abusive Father gave me some horrific negative I AM statements. Some of the more acceptable ones to publish were, *"Your birth ruined my life"* and *"You will never make anything of your life"* and *"Why can't you be like other people's children?"*

Unbeknown to me, these statements were playing in my ear every day of my life, thanks to my parrot. They were showing up in all aspects of my life. They were not doing me any favours because they affected my self-esteem and confidence. As a result, my parrot turned me into an angry person who blamed everyone and everything. To be honest, this angry person was not doing too much with his life.

I do not have that identity now because of one thing. Morning and evening, out loud I say a set of positive I AM statements. I speak them so loudly and so passionately that I have started to believe them over the years. This new identity has led to new behaviours, and ultimately better results in my life. The real trick is that you have to say these I AM statements out loud. You cannot do them in your head. You must verbalise them and verbalise them with as much passion and volume as you possibly can. When you do them, you must believe them; you must feel a real force within you when you say them.

Once you start doing this regularly, you will slowly begin to believe what you say at a deep and personal level. This will slowly start to change your identity and over time your behaviours will change.

For reference, my I AM statements have changed over time, but here are some of the ones I will always use:

- I AM a beautiful person
- I AM lovable

- I AM a great husband
- I AM a great father
- I AM a great business owner

Mohammed Ali, the most famous sportsperson to ever walk the planet, kept repeating, *"I am the greatest."* He repeated it so much that soon he started to believe it. This identity changed his behaviours to the extent that he is rightly known as the greatest heavyweight boxer of all time.

This principle is something I teach all my clients. As you can imagine, when I first explain the principle, I get some strange looks! Yes, it is a little *"far out,"* especially for us, stuffy Brits. But if ever the principle of participation and giving things a go was needed, it is here. I am so sure that saying I AM statements out loud with conviction and vigour will make a difference in your life. Please try.

One sceptical client raised a good point. She asked, *"What will happen if I genuinely do not believe in the I AM statements I make?"* I asked her to start her statements with the words; I AM IN THE PROCESS OF BECOMING A .... Remember, when you say them out loud, you must believe them. You must feel them burning inside you when you say them. Saying the I AM statements increases confidence and establishes self-esteem.

I have two daughters, and all the current research shows that females will suffer more from self-esteem issues than males. I do not know how old you are. I am 47 at the time of writing this book. I believe it is much harder for kids growing up now than it was when I was growing up. I do not want to argue about kids going down pits, healthcare, and general living standards back in the old days. But I believe it is harder for kids now because of technology, especially mobile devices, and social media. When I fell on my backside in the playground, which happened surprisingly often, everyone laughed for a while, and then it was forgotten. Now, there is a permanent reminder on the internet for the entire human race to see forever in a few minutes. These poor kids cannot get away from it. My trick has been to get my daughters to practice positive; I AM statements since they could first speak. I am not saying it is going to make a difference. But I hope that this process will give them the core identity to help them navigate the choppy waters of modern life. Time will tell.

Since Jan 2007, when I began Coaching professionally, I have been blessed to have had the benefit of so much personal development. I have helped so many people with the tools I have at my disposal. Of course, I will share those tools with you too. Yet, if I only had 30 seconds to give someone the most crucial bit of advice, it would be this. Twice a day out loud with such volume and passion that your jugular vein bulges, recite positive I AM statements. When you start to believe them, it will change your life!

Giving Things a Go

Have you ever been getting ready to go out on a Saturday night with friends? You look outside at the pouring rain and severe cold. Did you ever think how nice it would be to get a takeaway and cuddle up on the sofa with the fire on and watch trash TV with the family? No? That must just be me then! But, you go out and have a great time, and you are glad you went.

In life, things will not happen by magic. You need to act if you want something to happen. Warren Buffet, one of the wealthiest people on earth, says that the only difference between him and the next person is that he gives things a go. Does Warren Buffet always make the correct decisions? No, of course, he doesn't. But in his own words, he says, *"When I make a good decision, I make lots of money. When I make a bad decision, I make lots of learnings."* If Warren Buffet sat on his hands and did nothing, what would he get? It is not a trick question.

The principle of *"showing up"* and giving things a go is vital in life. You might not get the result you were looking for, but something will happen because of your actions. When you throw a pebble into a pond, it creates a ripple effect on the surface. The ripple effect is known as the Law of Precession. This law states that there is an effect at 90 degrees to where the initial impact took place. The ripples are at 90 degrees to the where the pebble hit the water. Not only will you hopefully get a result where you aim, but you will also get something happening at 90 degrees to that too.

The thing to remember is that nothing will happen if you do not act. After all, you cannot steer a parked car.

Things will happen if you act. Far too often, people are waiting for things to happen instead of taking control and doing something about it. Think about how many times you have not participated. How different would your life be if you had?

I see this a lot when people try something new, especially with marketing. As soon as it does not work, it is too easy to give up. Scrap that; it does not work! When all it needed was a little perseverance, and voila, you achieved the result you desired. There is an excellent story in Napoleon Hill's timeless classic, *"Think and Grow Rich."* He tells an account of the man who, during the gold rush, sold everything he had to buy a gold mine in Colorado. After months of digging, he had found nothing but dirt. Thoroughly dejected, and down to his last few cents, he sold his mine and all his equipment to a scrap metal dealer. After digging for 3 feet, the scrap metal dealer struck gold! How many times have we stopped 3 feet short because we did not take part and give things a go?

Fear

Everyone fears something. Am I scared of what other people may think of me if I succeed or fail? Am I scared of losing everything? Am I scared of employing people? Fear shows up for everyone, and if you are not careful, it will cripple you. Along the walkway of life, walls of fear will appear. When faced with these walls, some will look at them, decide that they seem like too much hard work, and retreat into their comfort zones. Some, however, will understand that the universe does not grant success to everyone. These walls of fear are the universe's way of only giving success to those who are prepared to scale those walls because they deserve it.

Back in January 2007, I launched my Business Coaching business. My first marketing strategy was a direct mail letter, followed by a call from me. I offered each recipient a free session with me to see if I could help them in their business. I have never been so far out of my comfort zone in all my professional life than when doing those follow-up calls. Telemarketing is such a hard job. Based on my experiences making those follow-up calls, I am never rude when receiving a cold call. I know how hard that person works.

My fear was rejection. No one likes rejection. I also had to deal with people being rude as I had disturbed them. It was a tough time. I realised however that if I could just make enough calls to get to speak to the business owners, I would make some appointments. If I managed to get the appointments, I trusted my sales system to get the client to sign up to work with me. I also knew that if I signed enough clients, my wife Angela would be able to leave her job and join me in the business. I was blessed to be married to someone more comfortable doing those follow up calls! I made the calls, got the appointments, and made the sales, and we never looked back.

Unfortunately, I saw too many other people in the franchise who could not get over the fear of picking up the phone and consequently lost their businesses. They did not pass the universe's test. The next time you feel fear, and it is holding you back, rationalise the emotion by using the FEAR acronym:

- **F**alse
- **E**xpectations
- **A**ppearing
- **R**eal

You see, when you do what you were terrified about, it is never as bad as you thought. Your mind, especially the negative voice in your head (the parrot on your shoulder), scares you to paralysis. You need to get past this as it has the power to destroy your business and your life. Look around at other people who are doing what you are scared to do. Tell yourself, *"If they can do it, then surely, so can I!"*

When I get scared, I ask, *"What is the worst that can happen?"* Well, in my opinion, the worst thing that can happen is that I die. If that is not likely to happen, then I am okay with that. I am more likely to overcome the fear that I am feeling because anything that does happen is better than being dead!

Work on YOU

Would you like to earn more? Well, if you do, you need to learn more. There is a direct correlation between learning and earning. Your learning ceiling will also be your earning ceiling. Too many people think that education finishes at school, college, or university, but education is lifelong. A big part of my coaching ensures my clients continue to learn through books, audiobooks, DVD's, or courses. By the way, one of the best ways of learning is observing others, especially kids!

I am not giving you a target of how many books to read, but as the saying goes, you add £500 to your annual salary for every book you read. If you are going to learn, then please keep notes. You will retain 30% more information if you make notes and refer to them. This way, you can also revert back to the notes you made on each book you read, rather than have to read the entire book again. Learning makes you ask better questions; it provokes more advanced thoughts and grows your brain. The most successful people I know are the best students. This positive correlation cannot be a coincidence.

Comfort Zone

Your business is a direct reflection of you, the leader. If you are stagnating, so is your business. If you lack focus, so does your business. If you lack discipline and motivation, so does your business. If you are not growing, neither is your business. One area that business owners need to get clear on is their growth. Your business is either growing or dying. All your growth comes outside of your comfort zone. It is meant to feel uncomfortable. It is meant to be scary. We are meant to make mistakes. The challenge we face is how we can force ourselves outside of our comfort zone. Very few people can do it, which is why I believe that everyone should have a Coach.

Stepping outside of your comfort zone is not something you can do once and think you have it licked. When you stretch an elastic band, it reverts to its original place the moment you let go. That is exactly what we do too. The moment we stop stretching, we revert to our comfort zones. We must keep stretching until we go past the point of elasticity and then the change will become permanent. I have coached some people for over ten years, and every two weeks, when they visit my office, they sit in the same chair! Human behaviour is so incredibly powerful to observe!

I see the real magic happen when people step out of their comfort zones on their own. As we know, this rarely happens. What usually happens is that people do not have a choice, and this scenario leads them to action. Remember, necessity is the mother of invention. Why is it that most businesses have their genesis in a recession? Maybe because so many people lose their jobs and have no choice. So, when was the last time you went outside of your comfort zone? Remember, if you grow, so will your business.

Pressure Power

In the old days before electric kettles, when we wanted to make a cup of tea, we would typically put a pan or kettle on the gas stove. We lit the match, and the flame appeared. This flame applied pressure (heat) to the water in the pan. After a while, tiny little bubbles would appear at the bottom of the pan. Under the surface, this water was now beginning to simmer. After a while, the pressure (heat) increased; the tiny

Mind Mastery

bubbles left the bottom of the pan, rose through the water, reached the surface of the water, and popped. The water changed from the liquid state to the gas state. The only reason this happened was because of the constant pressure.

Now let us talk about humans. They are already working hard. Maybe they read this book and start to think of all the things they need to do to improve their business. Under the surface, they may begin to simmer. If they begin to apply some of the book's learnings, the high temperature they feel might cause them to turn down the heat by putting the book down. Or worse still, they may throw the book away. If they do that, their temperature will cool, and they will go back to exactly where they were before. You must keep the heat on to force change. Keep going!

No significant change can happen without the application of positive pressure. Are diamonds not formed when tremendous pressure is applied? Let me qualify this immediately by stating I am not talking about negative pressure. Most of us refer to negative pressure as stress in its conventional sense. I am not going there in any way, shape, or form. What I am talking about is a healthy, positive pressure that forces us to act and to grow. Typically, most people (99.5%) need someone else to do this to them, a Coach.

I call this positive pressure, *"perturbation."* The word comes from the state of being perturbed. It is this state of perturbation that you need to endure more because it is where the magic happens. Remember, if you grow, so does your business. Every time you feel perturbed, remember, you are growing because of it, and you will learn so much about your resilience. At the time of writing, we are currently in lockdown during Covid-19. It is fair to say that many business owners will learn lots about themselves when they review this period. Hopefully, they will find that they grew because of the terrible situation we all faced.

Another way of looking at perturbation is the transformation of a caterpillar into a butterfly. When a caterpillar goes through perturbation, it would not be a pretty sight if you were to look inside the chrysalis. It would be a horrible gooey mess. The same happens with a human. When they are going through perturbation, it is not a pretty sight. Once a caterpillar becomes a butterfly, it does not go back to being a caterpillar. Perturbation is irreversible. Once it is a butterfly, it can do so much more than a caterpillar. Perturbation leads you to higher levels of productivity. So, the next time you feel the strain ask yourself, *"Is this perturbation?"* If it is, hang in there until your breakthrough catapults you to the next level. If you do, your business will also grow.

Mind Mastery

Success from Setbacks

Setbacks will happen. Straight lines do not exist. People have a romantic notion that everything will be a bed of roses. The romantic idea of a business without setbacks is the reason most people do not handle them well. Business owners should expect setbacks. The graphic below shows the reality of business and life.

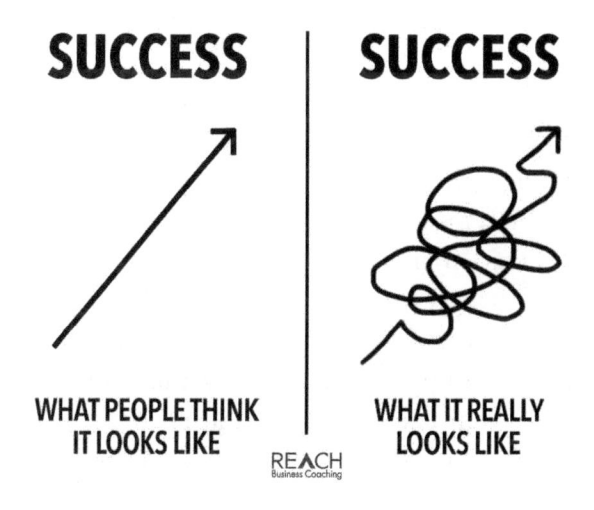

SUCCESS | **SUCCESS**

WHAT PEOPLE THINK IT LOOKS LIKE | WHAT IT REALLY LOOKS LIKE

REACH
Business Coaching

You will always have times when things do not go according to plan. It is how we deal with setbacks that determines our success. The slide below is a classic illustration of how we can use setbacks as a massive opportunity. See Appendix 5 at www.theeeplan.com.

45

Are you above

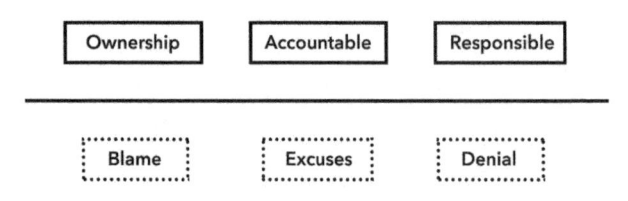

| Ownership | Accountable | Responsible |

| Blame | Excuses | Denial |

or below the line?

When things go wrong, far too many people engage in below the line behaviours. They blame everyone and everything else. They make excuses for what has gone wrong. And most of the time, they are in denial about the fact that anything is wrong! When you are below the line having what I call a *"pity party,"* what are you fixing about what has just gone wrong? Nothing! You are fixing nothing. Instead, you waste your number one asset, your energy, ranting and raving about how bad life is. Do you know anyone that is always below the line? Have you ever been below the line yourself? Of course, you have! It is natural. It is also impossible to live 100% above the line 100% of the time. If you do manage it, please let me know your secret!

The real learning about setbacks is this. When something happens that was not supposed to, the healthiest and wealthiest question you can ask is, *"So what am I going to do about it?"* The real focus in that sentence needs to be on the word *"I."* Do not focus on anyone else. By asking that question, when things go wrong, you will transform your culture and your

Mind Mastery

life. Print this slide. Make it visible everywhere, even at home, and refer to it all the time. The aim is to reduce the amount of time you spend below the line. Imagine when your team members start holding each other accountable to this slide ? Imagine when we tell our customers that no matter what has gone wrong, we will fix it? Imagine how this would feel? It will set you apart from everyone else. You and your business will fly because everyone else does pretty much the opposite of this.

Every setback is an opportunity to learn. I know that when it all goes wrong in the heat of battle, that is not how you think, but it is an unavoidable truth. Things either happen to you or for you. It depends on your mindset. Which lens do you view the world through? Victim, or victor? I find it to be true that most successful people have the mindset that views setbacks as opportunities to learn. So, whenever anything goes wrong, ask yourself, *"What is the opportunity here?"* I promise you that there will always be learnings there for you if you look at things this way.

One of my closest friends suffered the heartbreak of seeing his first child, stillborn. The pain my friend and his wife went through and continue to go through is something I cannot imagine. Yet, one day my friend's wife said something so humbling that I will take it to my grave. She said that if it was not for their first child dying, then they might not have had the opportunity to have the three beautiful children they now have. Please, ponder that for a moment. If a mother who gave birth to a stillborn baby can say that, what excuse can any of us have not to view setbacks as an opportunity? We can follow her example. We can consider any setback as a blessing and a chance to learn.

For Things to Change, First I Must Change

Change nothing, nothing changes. As mentioned in the previous section, the healthiest way to view any situation, good or bad, is to look for the opportunity. We have all been in dark places. There have been times when you did not know what to do. It may have seemed like an impossible situation. For my dad, this was so true. The fog may have descended to such a point that he could not see his hands in front of his face, never mind the next steps to take. If you ever face that situation, all you need to remember is this, *"For things to change, first, I must change."*

By realising this, you remove 359 degrees of opportunities to blame others and *"fix"* them. All you need to do is look at yourself instead. I cannot put into words the liberation I felt upon understanding that statement. Close your eyes and think for one minute that all the issues you face have solutions currently residing within you. Isn't that mind-blowingly powerful?!?

You do not need to know what the answer is. You don't even need to know what the question is. You just need to know that it is within you. With faith and looking inward, ask yourself, *"What can I do differently?"* Then, and it might not happen immediately, the answer will appear. You will achieve all your objectives and live an abundant life. Understanding *"for things to change, first*

I must change" has altered the entire course of my life! I cannot stress enough the importance of understanding this one concept.

CHAPTER 5

TIME MASTERY

A wise man once said, *"You can make a million pounds, and you can lose a million pounds, but nothing is stopping you from making it back in the same lifetime."* Yet, if you waste a second of your time, you cannot get it back, making time more valuable than money. Time is the one thing that we receive the same amount of every day, but some people use it better than others. Why?

Your Relationship with Time

What is your relationship with time? Do you see it as easy come, easy go? Do you let people waste your time? Do you waste the time of others? Are you always late? Your relationship with time will affect how you implement the time mastery strategies I am about to give you. I ask my clients to become ruthless with their time. I want them to view time as the precious resource that will determine their success. Focus on performing the £500 per hour jobs instead of the £8 per hour ones. Protect your time with everything you have. Do not let people casually take it away from you. Remember, it is you that is letting people take it from you. Remember, poor people spend time to save money; rich people spend money to save time. These

Time Mastery

rich people understand that time is more valuable than money. They are rich because of this mindset.

Deceptive Distractions

Without a doubt, one of the biggest drains on our time, especially in this modern connected world we live in, is distractions. A recent study calculated that we waste over 65% of our time because of distractions. That is not a typo. Two-thirds of the time we have available to move our businesses to profitability is lost because of distractions. Wow!

Imagine you are engrossed in creating your monthly profit and loss statement. Someone comes to your desk and asks, *"What do you want for lunch?"* It is not the answer, *"a sandwich please,"* that takes your time, it is the *"now, where was I?"* when you go back to your task. The inability to complete one job without distraction kills about two-thirds of your time. Imagine how much more you could do with your business and your life if you could stop this drain of your time? I hope you are feeling pained enough to want to deal with this.

Distractions come from people in three principal formats:

1. **Email** – Who was around before email? Business still got done. Somewhere along the way, we have become a slave to email, and instead of it serving us, we serve it. Again, imagine working on that profit and loss and the email notification pings. You go and check it immediately. Hands up if you're

guilty of this? You realise the email was more junk and delete it. You go back to the P&L, and "now, where was I?" Can you see how this is crippling your ability to do your job?

My solution is one that makes people's heads spin. It is so controversial that it should come with a Government health warning. Hang on to your hats, folks, "Switch off your email!" Most people respond, "What? Are you mad? I cannot do that! The world would stop spinning on its axis if I switched off email and did not respond within a nanosecond!" I am not saying switch it off permanently. My most successful clients only check emails three times a day. They check morning, midday, and end of the day. They tell their contacts this by having it on their email signature and an autoresponder saying, "I check emails at 9 am and 12:30 pm and 4 pm. If your inquiry is urgent, please call me." If it was urgent, they should have called, right??? For reference, my client's contacts tell them this is a great idea and start doing the same! If you cannot trust yourself not to check emails, then ask your IT people to only switch on Send/Receive at those times. Regardless of how you go about stopping being driven by your email, you need to do something about this modern-day distraction.

2. **Face to Face** – For me, this is the most destructive because it affects more than just

Time Mastery

you. "Have you got a minute?" How many times a day do your people ask you this? And how many times a day does it end up being just a minute? Every time you receive a question and answer it, you continue to drive the culture of dependability on you. I know why you started off giving the answers. It is because you are a good person and you want to help your people. You do not want the customer to be let down. I get that. But, if you do not address this distraction, you are destined to answer questions all day, every day. Just as harmful is the fact that your people will not grow because you stop them from thinking for themselves. The "just ask the boss" culture in your office is destructive to all parties. When team members ask you a question, is it not true that they already know the answer nine times out of 10? They have just become conditioned to ask you because you let them. You may have superstars right under your nose in your team. But all you do is answer their questions and stop them from thinking. You stop them from growing and achieving their full potential. Remember, just like you, as your people grow, so does the business. Most times, you being visible is the reason team members do not take the initiative and think for themselves. How about not being so visible all the time?

So, how do you deal with this "ask the boss" culture? After all, you don't want your people to think they can't come to you. Firstly, you must tell your teams that you have let them down. You tell them that you have not let them grow and develop. Every time they had a question, you answered it. Humility is a massive quality in leadership. Show it. Tell your team that from now on, every time they come to you with a question, you want them to give you two possible answers. You want them to have the opportunity to solve the issue. If they do not give you two possible suggestions, then you will not listen to their question, let alone answer it. Overnight your distractions from your people will disappear because they already know the answer. Your people will grow and develop, and you can get on with your £500 per hour jobs. You must also get better at answering questions with questions. For example, the next time you are asked a question, how about replying with: "What would you do if I was not here?" "What did you do the last time this happened?" "If you had to decide on what to do, what would it be?" This approach may be awkward in the beginning, but I promise you it gets easier. So, the next time someone asks you a question, start practising replying with questions.

3. **Phone** – When you are working on a £500 per hour job, leave your phone away from you. Some people tell me that they will have

Time Mastery

their phone on silent next to them. That does not work because you will still see it. When you realise it is your most significant customer calling, you will answer it, and you will have lost the opportunity to achieve more with your time. Remember, I am not saying you need to have it switched off all day, just for an hour or even 30 minutes at a time. You will get the important things done without distractions.

A Boss Myth

When it comes to belief systems, this can be one of the hardest to shift. I hear, *"But I am the boss Jas. I need to set a good example and be there all the time."* At REACH Business Coaching, our vision is *"To give every business owner a business to be proud of, and a life worth living."* One of our core values is *"Balance."* If you cannot incorporate *"balance"* into your belief system, you are destined to work every possible hour. You will miss out on doing the things you want to do with your life, especially with your family. And you will die young! What a crying shame, and what a waste. Undoubtedly, while you are here, it makes sense to enjoy life and live it?

Entrepreneurs drive the economy, not governments. It is entrepreneurs who create jobs for people. Entrepreneurs should be good role models for their team members and their kids, who should feel inspired to go into business. They will not dare go into business if they see their boss or parent working all hours, miserable, stressed, and close to a nervous breakdown.

Some business owners wear *"working hard"* as a *"badge of honour."* There is a strongly held belief system here that the boss must work the hardest and make the most sacrifices, including not seeing their families. Let me tell you something that breaks my heart. These business owners come from a scarcity mindset that says you either have a business or a life. Why not have a business and a life? That is the *"abundant"* mindset I teach. The real crazy secret I share with my clients is that I want them to be lazy. I want them to think lazy and be lazy, especially when thinking about the mundane low-level tasks that they should not do. You should do everything in your power to avoid these tasks like the plague so that you can spend your time doing the £500 per hour jobs. So that you can see your kids or whatever else you would like to do.

Many people ask me how I have so many successful businesses and still finish work at 4 pm. They are normally disappointed in my answer. I feel they expect an in-depth and detailed reply outlining the exact processes I go through daily. They want to know the tools I use to get so much done in such a relatively short space of time. The answer they receive is that I finish at 4 pm every day because I choose to. There it is. I simply decide to finish at 4 pm. I decided that when I started my first business. I wanted to make sure I was there for my daughters at breakfast and after school. Indeed, the thing I feel blessed with over everything else I have achieved in business so far has been that I have been there for my family every time. So, decide not to work all the time. Be resolute in that goal, and then get to work to make it happen.

Most business owners worry about what their teams will think if they are not first in and last out. The first point is, if anyone in your team has an issue with you not working 25 hours a day, eight days a week, they should not be in your team. The second point is, you deserve a life too!

Environment

We are the result of our environment; therefore, it makes sense to change our setting when we perform £500 per hour jobs. Open-plan offices help communication and teamwork, but they are a nightmare for working without distraction. How many times a day are you drawn into random conversations?! Once you have heard them, you are distracted. So, you need a separate space away from the distractions. Then you can take yourself off to this quiet space when you need to focus on the critical things.

A client of mine confessed that when he set up his business, the control freak in him ensured that his desk was in the middle of everybody else's in the office. It was his way of ensuring that he stayed on top of everything. What a mistake! Soon after starting to work with me, I raised his awareness to the point where he realised that he had to change something. He invested a couple of thousand pounds in creating a little office in the open-plan office corner. He now had a sanctuary to go to every day to ensure he had the couple of hours he needed to move his business forwards. The results were incredible, and he never looked back. I am not saying lock yourself in a room and detach yourself from everyone and everything. I am saying that you need a more private workspace for a couple of hours a day.

Those of you in open-plan offices have more of a challenge to avoiding distractions. Some creative things my clients have done to prevent distractions when working on £500 per hour jobs have included:

- Wearing a bright yellow hard hat.
- Putting on headphones.
- Putting a flag on their computer screen.
- Turning their back on the team and facing the wall for an hour.

Do anything you can to signal to people that this is *"Do Not Disturb"* time. So, where can you go to ensure you have the right environment once a day to get things done?

Multitasking Does Not Work

Women may say, *"Trust a man to say that!"* It is true; multitasking does not work. When was the last time you did six things at the same time? Did any of them come to completion? More than likely, you had to go back to them and finish them off properly, one by one, thus requiring even more time. A recent study has found that a staggering 28% of your time is lost because you try, and fail to multitask. Putting it another way, that is more than an entire quarter of a calendar year. Every four years, you lose a full year of productivity because you cannot discipline yourself to do one task at a time! What could you do to move your businesses and lives forwards if you had another quarter a year? What if your competitors have discovered that multitasking does not work and have an entire quarter a year more than you? What do you need to do to stop trying to juggle six balls in the air and to concentrate on dealing with one at a time?

Frogs

"Eat That Frog" is the title of one of the best books you could ever read on time mastery. Brian Tracy talks about how we tend to put off the horrible things on our *"to-do"* lists. We will find a million other things to do to avoid that terrible thing. Things like calling that customer complaint, chasing that person for payment, or calling that person to explain why you have not paid them. You will know what I refer to, and you also know how these tasks hang over you all day like a dark cloud. They sap your energy and fill you with anxiety. Eat that frog for breakfast means you should deal with the most significant, scariest, most revolting task first. That way, you can free yourself up of the dread and fear of thinking about it all day. You can focus on moving forwards with that burden taken off you.

Monkeys

"The One Minute Manager Meets the Monkey" is another excellent read that I recommend to anyone who wants to get better at using their time. In this book, Ken Blanchard talks about how people can give you their *"monkeys,"* which are typically their tasks that you end up taking on. It starts when someone approaches you and asks, *"Have you got a minute?"* The most significant way you end up taking other people's

"monkeys" is, after they explain to you their issues, you say something like, *"Let me think about it."* Now, you have that monkey on your back. That monkey, with the other monkeys you get handed, will weigh you down and grind you to a halt. As I mentioned before, think lazy and put those monkeys back on other people's backs by asking questions like, *"So what do you think we should do?"* Finish by saying, *"Come back to me at the end of the day with your solution."* Remember, think lazy.

Say NO!

The most powerful word in time management is *"no."* How easy do you find it to say that word? For most people, it is almost impossible to say because they feel as if it's their responsibility to help their people. It is as though saying *"no"* is a dereliction of duty. As I have said before, if you keep answering their questions, they will keep asking them.

Years ago, in one of my corporate roles, we launched a new product, which had been a massive success. The company did not prepare for the number of enquiries we received from prospective customers. I was given the task of training the entire team of over 500 people to help deal with the influx of enquiries. I would train the Team Leaders, and they would then have the skills necessary to field questions from their teams. Despite arming the Team Leaders with the information, I still fielded questions from most of the company. It got so bad that the management of my own team suffered. It got to the point where my Manager mentioned to me his concerns. He said, *"If the management of your team does not improve, then there might be repercussions on you."* At that point, I realised it was *"them or me."*

I was not going to lose my job for anyone! This experience gave me the necessary focus to begin turning away questions. I re-directed enquiries to the individual's Team Leader I had already trained. Upon returning to their own Team Leaders, the individuals found the answers they were looking for. Was it difficult to turn someone away the first time they came to me? It cut me to pieces, and I felt awful for not helping them. It went against all my beliefs. However, if I had not, then I dread to think what that might have meant to my future employment prospects. So, you now need to think like that too. You need to ask, *"what could happen to my business if I do not do the £500 per hour jobs because I am too busy answering questions?"*

Proactive vs. Reactive

Most business owners chase their tails 24/7. Most days finish with them asking, what did I achieve today? Does this frustrated state ring a bell with you? The rule of thumb that I work towards is that for every 1 minute I spend being proactive, I will save 10 minutes having to be reactive. Something as simple as having all the team together for 5 minutes first thing in the morning will, on average, save at least 50 minutes during the day. You will not have to remind people separately. This 5-minute *"huddle"* also improves communication and camaraderie.

If you always field questions, then how about having a weekly meeting where the team can bring all their issues and concerns? In the future, when people do bring you questions, and after asking for two possible answers, ask them if it can wait until their weekly catch up with you. People become conditioned to write a list to bring to their weekly catch up. Better still, they start to realise, upon writing the list, they already know the answer and do not need your help after all.

Parkinson's Law

If you give a human being 2 hours to do a task, they will take 2. If you give them 4, they will take 4. And if you do not provide them with a deadline, god help you! How much more do you get done on the day you break up for your holiday? Loads more, of course, because you have a deadline, you do not have a choice. The issue on all other days is that business owners have a choice; they do not have deadlines. Most businesspeople let things drift into all parts of the day, and unfortunately, the night. *"It'ss okay; I will do this tonight, or at the weekend."* No! That is not the right way of creating a healthy work-life balance. What would happen if you could not work past 5 pm? You would get the work done, of course. You would become ultra-efficient, kick back on distractions, and become ruthless with your time. All this would happen because you did not have a choice. They say that necessity is the mother of invention, so make it necessary that you MUST finish work at 5 pm. A little trick to use is to have something you must go to after work that you cannot miss. This should focus the mind on ensuring you finish on time.

Law of Vacuum

Have you ever had a situation where an appointment in your diary got cancelled at short notice? You thought to yourself, *"Great, I will get loads of other stuff done now!"* Then you turn around 4 hours later, and you have got nothing done. Well, that is because you did not account for the Law of Vacuum. The Law of Vacuum states that nature abhors a vacuum. A vacuum cannot exist. So, when a cancelled appointment creates a vacuum in your diary, fill it with a £500 per hour job, or nature will fill it with lots of £8 per hour jobs.

One thing that gives me immense pride is that my most disciplined clients have *"Gym"* as an entry in the working day in their Default Diaries (more on Default Diaries later). You see, if they had not gone to the gym, their teams no doubt would have filled that time with needless £8 per hour jobs. A less disciplined person would think they would go to the gym at the end of the day instead, which would mean missing out on family time or something else. But my clients are disciplined enough to understand this, so they stick to the slot they have in their Default Diary.

Years ago, a client realised that he was wasting approximately 20 hours per week on basic administration. He acted and hired a full-time Office Administrator on an annual salary of £20k. A few months later, he cut a frustrated figure because he still had not managed to find time for the £500 per hour jobs. He felt like he was still chasing his tail all day. He had not filled the time in his diary that he had saved with the new hire with something productive, and as such, nature-filled it for him. Except now he was also paying someone £20k per year too! So, next time you have a gap in your diary, what activities will you plug into the time slot?

There Is More Than Enough Time

The mind can play tricks on you. As we have said before, mindset drives 100% of what happens to you. In the past, I had always felt that becoming involved in more business ventures would mean less time at home with Team Darar. I can hand on heart say that this has limited my progress. Then, I tried this trick. I told myself with absolute conviction that there was more than enough time. This one shift in mindset or belief system increased my productivity by at least 100%. This change has been profound. I share this trick with you, hoping that it can also help you identify where you are wasting time. And how you can use wasted time to do so much more. Remember, there's more than enough time.

Delegation

If a job is worth doing, you may as well do it yourself. How many times have you heard that or said it yourself? At some stage, we have all done this. Yet, I want to question this because it is another belief system that will prevent you from achieving Time Mastery.

I have found that people do not or will not delegate to other people because, in the past, someone let them down. Thus, they now have a complete block when

Time Mastery

it comes to asking others to do some usual £8 per hour *"stuff"* for them. They just do it themselves and consequently are destined to do it forever.

Delegation is about writing a system, training it out, delegating it, and then periodically checking compliance. This process takes more time at the front end but will save you so much time in the long run. Your team feels empowered because you trusted them, and you have lost some £8 per hour jobs and have time for some £500 per hour jobs. WIN:WIN!

Let me qualify this by stating that there is a massive difference between delegation and abdication. Abdication is when you ask or tell someone to do something when you feel super stressed because you do not have the time to do it. Abdication NEVER works and will always come back to bite you.

Time Study

Doing a time study is something I ask all my clients to do, and I invite you to do the same. Create a spreadsheet like the one in Appendix 6. You can download the document at www.theeeplan.com.

If your working day starts before 7 am and ends after 6 pm, then just adapt this sheet accordingly. Next, print out 10 of these. For the next ten working days, log what you do every 15-minutes. It is incredibly hard to do, and will need tremendous discipline.

When doing the time study, you must follow these two golden rules:

- **Golden Rule 1** – You must do this in real-time. Some people think they can cheat the system and log their actions at the end of the morning, for example. Well, I hope you will agree with me that most of us cannot remember what we did 30 seconds ago, never mind what we did 3 hours ago! Please, do it in real-time. You will undoubtedly have to use technology such as a diary reminder every 15 mins or a phone reminder every 15 mins to ensure you log your actions every 15 minutes. If you are driving, please do not stop every 15 minutes! And if you are in a meeting, do not pause every 15 minutes; just do that at the end! Log everything else in real-time every 15 minutes.

- **Golden Rule 2** – You must do the time study with 100% honesty. If you have just spent half an hour checking the footie scores in readiness for your weekend accumulator, then put it down. If you lie, you are only lying to yourself.

When you have ten working days of time study sheets, bring them together and cut out all the 15-minute slots you have been filling in for the last ten days. On your desk will be a mass of thin strips of paper, like a pile of ticker tape. Place 6 to 8 buckets neatly in a line. Give each bucket a title of a key functional area in your business. The functional areas should include things like Sales, Marketing, Operations, Finance, and Admin. Please add another two buckets to the line, Miscellaneous and Time-Wasting.

Time Mastery

Now, pick up one strip of paper at a time, read it, and throw it into the bucket where it belongs. Do this with all the strips of paper from your time study. Because you have a Miscellaneous and Time-Wasting bucket, theoretically, your desk should be clear of all the strips of paper

Next, empty the buckets and tally up the total amount of time in each bucket. Write down the totals and begin analysing the results. Were there any shocks? What if next to each bucket, you have an hourly rate for that task? Are there things that you should not be doing? What could you delegate? This process can be a real eye-opener and becomes the first step to developing Time Mastery.

Rocks

Most folks have heard this story. If not, this story is just for you. During a lecture, a University Professor reaches underneath his desk and produces a glass jar. Carefully placing it on the desk, he reaches down and takes out three large rocks, which he gently puts into the jar. The third rock reaches the level of the top of the jar, and the Professor asks the class, *"Is this jar full?"* The students reply, *"Yes."* He then proceeds to bring from under the desk a bag full of small pebbles, which he pours into the jar, and these pebbles fill the gaps between the large rocks and reach the top of the jar. He now asks his class, *"Is this jar full?"* The students reply for the second time, *"Yes."* He then proceeds to bring out a bag of fine sand and pours this into the jar and fills all the remaining gaps, and reaches the top of the jar. Feeling immensely proud of himself, he asks the class, *"Is this jar full?"* The students reply for the third time, *"Yes!"* Finally, he gets a glass of water, pours it into the jar until everything overflows, and the jar is finally full.

The moral of the story is that if you do not put the rocks into the jar first, then the pebbles, sand, and water will stop them from going in. In our context, we are referring to the £500 per hour jobs as rocks, and the pebbles, sand, and water are the other £8 per hour *"stuff."* The jar is our diary. So, we need to put £500 per hour jobs into the diary first, and if there is space for the other £8 per hour *"stuff"*, great. Too often, it is the other way around for business owners. They do all the other £8 per hour *"stuff"* first and then run out of time to do the critical £500 per hour jobs. The thing to remember is that while the £8 per hour *"stuff"* could have been delegated and done by other people, the £500 per hour jobs cannot. If you do not do the £500 per hour jobs, no one does. Scary!

Going back to Eat That Frog, another concept that Brian Tracy talks about is the 80/20 rule. 20% of what you do makes 80% of the difference. So, it makes sense to ensure that 20% (the rocks) go in the diary first. If I can make Time Mastery simple, it would be this. For 2 hours a day, go in a room away from people, away from your phone, and with no email. Concentrate on doing one thing at a time to completion, and you will change your life. Too many people tell me that this is too simple a fix. I tell them that I am a simple person and choose simplicity over complication every day of

Time Mastery

the week. So, when will you grab control of your time and start driving the day instead of it driving you?

Default Diary

In all my time Coaching businesspeople just like you, this is the most important tool I can ever give you to manage your time better. Once I've explained it, you might think that it is so simple that it can't make that much of a difference. Please remember, simplicity is king.

The Default Diary principle is to put the critical *"rocks"* or £500 per hour jobs into your diary first, not last, or never like most business owners do. Most people tell themselves that they will do the important tasks when they have time to do them. As we all know, unfortunately, this means they never happen.

With the Default Diary, we put in the £500 per hour jobs first, and then the £8 per hour jobs can fill the rest of the space. This fundamental mindset shift is why the Default Diary is the most important tool I can ever give you to manage your time. See Appendix 6a at www.theeeplan.com for an example Default Diary.

Please note, this Default Diary took many years to create. If you decide to make one for yourself, please start with 2 or 3 *"rocks"* first. Get used to doing them, then slowly add one more rock at a time. The reason why a Default Diary won't work is that people put too much in, too quickly. You can't go from zero to hero in one step because your mindset, your team, your systems, and processes aren't ready for it. Do it slowly.

Please leave time for *"emergencies."* These happen to us all, and we need some time for these. If you fill your Default Diary up, with no time for *"emergencies,"* it won't be realistic, you'll find it impractical, and you'll stop using it.

Colour coding it and making it visible is also important as it trains your team to know when your *"do not disturb"* times are.

Most importantly, you have a straightforward tool that will ensure you get the most important things done that, if you don't do, no one else will.

CHAPTER 6

MONEY MASTERY

If you do not know the numbers, you do not know the score. If you do not know the score, you do not know if you are winning or losing. If you do not know if you are winning or losing, what is the point in playing the game?

When NASA flies to the moon, they do not fly in a straight line. They make upwards of 60,000 adjustments on the way. The NASA control centre makes adjustments based on the data they read, and I believe business owners need to make course corrections like NASA do. You adjust based on the readings you take. Unfortunately, for most people, Money Mastery is checking online banking every morning. For some, it is spending 43.2 seconds reading their Year End Accounts annually. For another group, it is ignoring the numbers and hoping that everything will be okay. None of these are acceptable because they do not allow you to adjust as you go along. I believe that numbers tell you what to do next, and if you know the numbers, you are so much better placed to drive your business forwards.

Money is the language of business, but unfortunately, most business owners cannot talk the language of business. Financials are that *"dark art,"* that *"black magic"* that Accountants do. Imagine a gigantic book so big and thick it would take two people to pick it up. That is the *"book"* our Accountants read. They spend years getting their qualifications by reading and understanding this *"book."* Accountants pass exams to show they fully understand this *"book."* Just for the record, this *"book"* does not exist. I am using it for effect, but I hope you get my point. Most Accountants will tell you that humble business owners like you and me only need to understand one page of this *"book."* We pay our great Accountants to do the rest. And if I can understand that one page, I am going to make sure you do too.

When writing this book, I have Coached over 3,000 businesses and have 3 of my own. With every one of these, I need a minimum of three documents to have confidence that I have Money Mastery. There are others, but if I have these three documents, I know that I can make significant decisions and safely steer the ship through choppy waters.

Profit and Loss

Every business should generate a Profit and Loss statement. You can find a template in Appendix 7 at www.theeeplan.com.

A P&L is not real. For a start, it does not include value-added tax (VAT) in monies coming in or out. It also is based on the accounting method you use. Primarily there is Cash-Based Accounting and Accrual Based Accounting. Cash-Based Accounting is where you register the cost or sale amount when the monies move from you or to you. Accrual Based Accounting is where you register the cost or sale based on the date an invoice is issued. For example, in Cash-Based Accounting, if we purchased four office chairs on 10th Feb and the supplier gave us 30 days terms, and we paid on 10th March, this cost would register in our accounts in March, because that's when the cash left us. In Accrual Based Accounting in the same example, the cost would register in our accounts in Feb because that is when the invoice was received. The same principle applies to incoming monies.

Your first job is to complete the Budget tab with your forecast of what you want to happen in these next 12 months. This is all about setting your Reticular Activating System (the GPS). Remember, this is a template, so feel free to add and subtract lines and headings to match your business. Start with your sales. If it exists, use your understanding of your seasonality here to be as accurate as possible with your forecast. Include other factors like increased marketing and sales activity to plot what you expect to happen over the next 12 months. Then comes the part that most people struggle with, the Cost of Sales. Here you list all the costs associated with selling your product or service. Some people call these Variable Costs or Direct Costs. These costs will fluctuate, depending on how busy or quiet you are. This total gives you your Gross Profit number. Finally, you complete the overheads. Most people understand this bit the most. This will then provide you with the net profit. Once you have done this Budget, you will have something that over 95% of business owners do not have, a theoretical picture of your business. For most of you, this is the first time you will have seen your business like this. For some of you, it will be a pleasant surprise, unfortunately, for others it might be a reality check that you desperately needed. In my experience as a Business Coach based on this Budget, I have had to tell several business owners to close due to trading while insolvent. I do not want to scare you, but it does happen from time to time. By creating this Budget, we can at least see how viable your business is.

Now you have your 12-month forecast in place. You have set your RAS on what you want to happen. You now need to take any headings you changed in column A on the Budget tab and transfer them to column A on the Actuals tab. Your job or a bookkeeper's job is to populate each month with actuals when the month has finished. Then, you compare these against the Budget. You can do this in the Profit Tracker tab or just toggle between Budget and Actual. Comparing the budget projections with the actuals gives you the ability to make adjustments, at the very least, monthly. So, based on the readings, what adjustments are you going to make to stay on track?

Cashflow Forecast

Unlike your P&L, the Cashflow forecast is real. It is like your bank statement. This is actual pounds and pennies coming in and out. Once again, you can find a template in Appendix 8 at www.theeeplan.com.

I use 13 weeks because it is incredibly hard to forecast any more than that when it comes to cash coming in and going out. So, first, you need to complete the Inflow tab with the amounts you expect to come in and when. You make your best guess. Then, complete the Outflow tab with the payments you predict to go out and when. Then, go to the Forecast tab. Type in your opening bank balance and overdraft limit, and you have your 13-week cash flow forecast. If you go into your overdraft, the closing weekly balance goes to a red font. But if you go past your overdraft, the closing weekly balance goes to a red font with a red background. This visual aspect is essential for you to see any issues and focus the mind on fixing them.

Unfortunately, most businesspeople wake up on the Monday morning of the red/red week, and it is too late to do anything about it. With the 13-week cashflow forecast, you can at least see if there is a red/red situation and have time to try and do something about it. A new client had this red/red situation several years ago when creating their first 13-week cash flow forecast. To our horror, it showed that in Week 9, we were red/red. Thankfully, we rolled our sleeves up and made some tough decisions. We let some of the team go and cut some costs while going into overdrive with marketing. I am pleased and relieved to report that the business is still here today. If we had not had this document, we would have only seen the situation in Week 9. We would not have had enough time to make changes. In all reality, we would have had to close the business down. If your business works on a longer cycle, for example, house building, you may consider a 12, or even 24-month cashflow forecast document. Regardless of what type of business you have, please start doing this and review if every week.

Dashboard

You cannot manage what you do not measure. The P&L and Cashflow forecast tell us about the financials. Every business however has a whole variety of other numbers that we need to keep an eye on too. If you walked into an A&E Dept in a Hospital and saw a patient surrounded by medical staff, that patient will be hooked up to machines. These machines are giving the medical staff readouts on how the patient is doing based on their treatment. The same applies to a Dashboard in a business. It gives us readouts to tell us if what we are doing has a positive or negative effect.

A Dashboard can take many forms. There are some fantastic cheap and sometimes even free software solutions out there. These software solutions will make displaying your Dashboard data even more impactful. To start with, I always recommend a basic Excel form. You will see many examples of Dashboards in Appendix 9 at www.theeeplan.com.

Dashboards always evolve, and the more you get into a culture of measuring everything, the more things you will add to the Dashboard. A real-life example of how we use the Dashboard came with a retail client several years ago. We wanted to know if hiring a full-time person to meet and greet customers would be cost-effective. We trialled it for two weeks with an

Money Mastery

existing team member to see what impact the person would have, particularly on how much money people spent. After the 2-week trial, we were able to see the average value sale uplift as a result of the customer having someone meet and greet them and to be there to show them around the shop. We already knew our average margin per transaction. So, the decision to hire someone to do this job full-time was easy because we could see that this person would more than pay their salary. Do not guess what to do next; use numbers to tell you what to do next.

In my experience, the Dashboard, with its continual evolution, gets too big. After a while you will need to condense it down. You need to keep all the data you are capturing, but maybe you create a cover sheet that will just give you the key numbers. After all, in a car, a Dashboard is something that we look down at for a split second to ensure that there are no flashing red lights.

Margins Analysis

In every business, different products and services make us varying amounts of profit. As most businesspeople do not have Money Mastery, they do not know what product or service makes what profit. A relatively simple exercise I ask my clients to undertake can have profound effects as it can give us real power to change things. Please see the Margins Analysis sheet in Appendix 10 at www.theeeplan.com.

In column B is the customer (there are some examples already in there). Column C is the price they paid. Column D is the actual cost to us. Column E is the difference (profit or loss). Column F is the margin in percentage terms. Column G is mark up in percentage terms. We will discuss the difference between margin and mark up next. In all my time, this exercise has not failed to make my clients say, *"Well, I didn't know that!"* It may be that either a customer has negotiated us down on price so much. It may be that suppliers' costs have gone up so much. In most instances, this exercise shines a light on where money has been leaking from the business with loss-making products and services. Should you not know what goes on under the surface of your business?

Margin vs. Mark-Up

It might come as a surprise to you that these are two different things. Far too often, I see business owners get these two things mixed up at a high cost to them. Margin is your profit as a percentage of your sale price, whereas mark-up is your profit as a percentage of your cost price. In the example, in Appendix 11 at www.theeeplan.com, you will see this illustrated.

In the first diagram the unit is sold for 100. The cost price is 80, meaning the profit is 20. 20 (profit) divided into 100 (sale price) is a 20% margin. In the second diagram the numbers are the same as the first diagram, but this time, we divide the 20 (profit) into the 80 (cost price) to get a 25% mark-up.

Where people can go wrong is where they get these the wrong way round, or worse still, they do not know there is a difference. Imagine a shop selling something for 100 and thinking there was a 25% margin instead of a 20% mark-up because they got mark-up and margin the wrong way round. Let us say they wanted to shift some slow-moving stock. So, they created a sale to sell things at cost price to get rid of it and free up some cash flow and space in the shop. Let us say they discounted 25% because they thought there was a 25% profit in it. Now, they are selling something for 75 when it cost 80. Instead of selling a product or service at the cost price, they sell it at a loss. You may need to read this a few times to get your head around it, but please do because this is something that you need to understand.

Chasing Money

An emotive subject for many business owners is the topic of debtors. Too often, they will not chase people who owe them money for fear of:

- Upsetting them.
- Affecting the relationship.
- Losing that customer's business in the future.

People pay the people who chase them the most. So, do you pursue the people who owe you money with the right level of energy? If money is the oxygen, and we cannot breathe without it, surely then, chasing debts is a priority? I believe that any business that gives terms should have a systemised and robust debtors process. Start with daily invoicing, not weekly or monthly, but daily. The clock is ticking. You need to start getting the oxygen back in. You need to make sure they have received the invoice as you do not want to find out that they have not received it after 30 days. Then, three days before the monies are due, you should contact them to ensure that everything is okay. If it is received, then send a thank you email. If you do not receive the money owed, then no grey area here. The debt now needs to move to the next stage.

You need to send professionally crafted emails/letters. If you do not receive the monies within the required timeframe, you need to pass the debt on to a specialist 3rd party. This escalation is no offence to you, but a Solicitor letter carries more power than yours. More and more Solicitors are now offering this service, and some charge only £15 per letter. For those debts that we need to write off, and then the customer comes back to us, the customer must pay 100% upfront.

Some say that they do not chase debts because they do not want to affect their relationships with their customers. Fine, I get that. Find someone else to pursue them. I have never once spoken to a client of mine about an invoice. For reference, we ask our clients to set up Standing Orders for the 1st day of every month for that months Coaching fees. We don't give terms.

For those one-person armies out there, who do not have anyone else to do this for them, then create another email address called Accounts@. Then, word emails as though they are from a 3rd party. Some Banks, Accountants, and Solicitors offer cost-effective Credit Control facilities. You can shift the burden away from you if you want to.

For those of you who deal with bigger businesses or work with the Public Sector, then please get to know on first name terms, the person(s) in the Accounts Department. At Christmas, send them a Christmas card and a box of biscuits (to share with the office to avoid any Bribery legislation). When you are in a hole, and your invoice is number 63 on their list, calling them up for help and using their first name might be the thing that saves your skin.

So, what do you need to do to ensure that the money comes back into you quicker?

Break-Even

Do you know your break-even point? If you think it is the total of your fixed costs, you would be sadly mistaken. The actual formula that I teach to calculate break-even is Fixed Costs/Gross Margin%. Knowing your break-even focuses the mind on what you need to do to ensure that you are getting your head above water. Remember, you cannot manage what you do not measure. So, do you need to calculate your break-even?

Terms and Conditions

It is too late to realise that your T&C's are not fit for purpose when you have a dispute. Far too often, I see people downloading T&Cs from the internet. Worse still, some people do not even have any! Please invest the money to instruct a Commercial Solicitor to draft your T&C's and ensure the Solicitor reviews them regularly for compliance. Indeed, one client of mine freely admits that not having robust T&Cs in place in his business has resulted in losses of over £50k a year. It makes sense to get this right!

Pricing for Profits

Without a doubt, pricing is one of the most contentious areas I must address when working with clients. The heartbreaking thing is that I could coach some people for years, and they still would not make any money. All because they have the wrong pricing strategy. Let me be clear; this is not about ripping customers off. It is about charging a fair amount for all the effort, stress, and challenges you go through to deliver a good product or service to your customers. You deserve to get paid for that. Most often than not, business owners have more of an issue with pricing than their customers do.

I come across so many people who have not put their prices up for several years. I ask them if, in that time, their costs have gone up, to which, of course, they reply *"yes."* Then they wonder why they have not paid themselves in over a year! You need to address this because if you do not, you will be out of business.

At www.theeeplan.com in Appendix 12 is a grid that shows you the effect of increasing your pricing, dependent on your existing gross margin. It shows you how many customers you can afford to lose and not be any worse off from a profit perspective. At the very least, this should help you rationalise the fears you may have of putting your prices up.

Money Mastery

If you have not put your prices up in over a year, you can put them up by 10% today, and several things will happen:
- You will lose approximately 1% of your customers. To make things better, these are "D" Grade clients!
- No one will even notice, let alone mention it.
- Some people will say, "I wondered when you were going to do that. I cannot believe you have stayed in business this long."
- You will get busier! Yes, it is true. How many of you can hand on heart say that you might have lost business by being too cheap? Perceived value still plays a massive part in the buying process.

The effect of a 10% price rise is an immediate 10% increase in net profit. You must take this kind of action. If you do not, you will continue to live hand to mouth and wonder why you do not have any money left to pay yourself at the end of the month.

The rule of thumb is that if less than 10% of your customers complain about your price, it means you are too cheap. If more than 10% of customers complain about our price, you are too expensive.

Years ago, a friend of mine coached a kitchen manufacturer. This gentleman was in his mid-fifties and had been running this business since he left school. He had literally worked his fingers to the bone and had never made a penny. Upon working with him, the

Coach told him he needed to put his prices up by 10% just to give himself a chance of making things work. He also told him about the 10% threshold of people moaning about the price.

Seven weeks later, during a coaching session, the client mentioned that more than 10% of people were now complaining about the price. The Coach was puzzled as we had put the prices up seven weeks ago. Why were more people complaining now, he thought? As it happened, the client had misheard the Coach. He thought the Coach had said raise your prices by 10% a week!!! After SEVEN weeks, when his price was nearly 100% higher than when he first started (10% per week compounded over seven weeks), more than 10% of people were complaining!!! When you have stopped laughing at the craziness of the story, just for one-minute think about how hard the client had made it on himself. For all previous years, he undercharged his customers. A note of caution: when you put your price up, do not apologise for it. Say it with absolute confidence.

On the flip side of this coin is discounting. You can do all sorts of crazy things to your business, but the one guaranteed way of killing your business is to discount. Again, in Appendix 12 at www.theeeplan.com, you can also see what happens when you discount. How many more sales do you need to do to recover the margin you just gave away? You will learn more about how to get away from discounting in the section on USP & Guarantee. But in the meantime, please remember price is what the customer pays; value is what they get. Educate your customers on the value you are giving them, not the price they are paying. If you just discount to win work, you are training your customers to always ask for a discount.

A client of mine owns a large furniture retail business. Traditionally the sales team had discounted to win work. When I began coaching him, we immediately focused on training the sales team on how to sell without discounting. We also contacted our suppliers and asked for free items we could give to customers as a bonus to get the sale. A classic example of this was cushions. For instance, if a customer were haggling on price for a sofa, we would allow the salesperson to *"throw in"* a couple of cushions to get the sale. The salesperson remembered to tell the customer the value of what they were getting for free too. Remember, these cushions cost us nothing. The effect of these actions and how they stopped us from discounting and protected our margin added more than six figures to this business's net profit.

Do you need to look at your prices, and do you need to stop discounting?

Charging for Everything You Do

I am staggered at how much some businesses give away for free. I am not advocating charging for oxygen, but like everything in life, it is about balance. Most times, the pendulum has swung too far one way, and you are out of balance.

Just by auditing all the things you give away, you usually find a lot of money. Also, when people receive something for free, they do not appreciate or value it. Why not make the change?

Specialise, Do Not Generalise

One way in which businesses lose money is by trying to be everything to everyone. They stock all manner of products and offer all services hoping that someone might buy one of them one day. Operating your business like this is wrong. You should become known as specialists and experts in a niche. People have hundreds of thousands of messages fired at them daily. If your message is trying to tell them about everything you do, it will get lost in the other *"noise."* Tell them about one thing, and they are more likely to remember. I know it might sound counter-intuitive, but my experience has shown me that niche wins every time.

An old client of mine had a shop on a busy main road. Outside the shop was a huge 30-foot sign that listed everything they did. One day, I got in a car with him and drove past his sign at 20mph. I asked him what he saw on the sign. He replied, *"Nothing."* When you tell people about everything, they remember nothing. When they do buy from you because they remembered the one thing, please feel free to tell them then about the other 8,391 items you sell.

CHAPTER 7

DELIVERY MASTERY

Business is simple. We make it complicated. Do what you said you were going to do when you were going to do it, and you will be world-class. How many companies do you deal with that do not do this? How many times has someone promised you a callback, an email, a quote, and it has not happened? Imagine if you could do this properly? Imagine how much you would outshine your competitors? Does it have to be any more complicated than this?

Consistency Wins Every Time

In an ever-changing world, people crave things to remain the same. That is why consistency in all our interactions with our customers is so important. Customers relate positively to a consistent experience every time. They use consistent experiences as a measure of customer satisfaction. McDonald's gets voted top of the class for customer satisfaction every time. How? They trust their customers so little they feel the need to screw the furniture to the floor in their restaurants. They do not serve you the most nutritionally beneficial food. And the customer service is not exactly world-class. How do they get voted so highly by their customers? It is because every time you buy from them, you know what is going to happen.

The Entrepreneur Escape Plan

Let us say I am new to a city. I moved there because of a new job. I need to get a haircut, and while walking down the street, I spot a nice-looking Gents Barbershop. I walk in, and upon entering the premises, the business owner immediately introduces himself and takes my name too. He leads me to a waiting area at the far end of the shop, which has two beautiful leather sofas and two armchairs. The waiting area has a flat-screen TV mounted on the wall above the couches, playing the 24 hours sports news channel. On a beautiful glass table in the middle of the sofas are four magazines covering cars, golf, football, and health. While I am waiting for my turn for my haircut, someone approaches me and hands me a drinks menu. Taken aback by such attention, I immediately revert to the default setting of a cup of tea. A few minutes later, my tea arrives in a bone china cup and saucer. A few minutes later, the business owner collects me as he will be cutting my hair today. When I arrive at his cutting chair, I notice that I have another cup of tea waiting for me, again, in a bone china cup and saucer. The business owner starts to shampoo my hair and, once washed, proceeds to cut my hair with scissors. He talks to me about his craft and explains why using scissors is better than electric clippers. I leave the establishment, having given a big tip and thinking what a great business that is.

Two weeks later, I return. As I walk in, no one comes to greet me, and I notice that the business owner is not there today. I make my way over to the waiting area where the TV is off, and there is only one magazine on the table. I am approached for my drinks order,

Delivery Mastery

and I order my standard cup of tea. This time my tea is served to me in a polystyrene vending machine cup. I am called over for my haircut and notice there is no refill cup of tea waiting for me. This time, the person cutting my hair does not wash it and uses electric clippers. I leave the business this time, feeling confused. How could it have been so different from the first time? Because the first time had been so good, however, I must go back because this could have just been an off day.

A fortnight later, I return. The business owner immediately introduces himself and takes my name. He takes me over to the waiting area where I notice that the TV is off and there are no magazines at all this time. No one comes to take my drink order, either. I am called over to the business owner's cutting station and notice that they have a glass of water waiting for me that I did not even order. This time, he does not wash my hair but uses scissors.

When exiting this business for the third time, 80% of customers will decide that they will not return because they do not know what will happen next time. The same 80% ratio applies to every customer of every business on earth. So, your challenge is to ask yourself, *"How consistent is the experience my customers have?"* Does it depend on the mood of the person serving them on that day? If it does, you will not deliver consistently and reliably every time. We need a system to ensure consistent delivery. Does everyone have the same uniforms? Is the greeting the same? Are your emails all sent using the same font? Do your company vehicles all look the same? This list is endless, but this is just a little something to get you thinking. I am not saying you need to be excellent; I am saying you need to be consistent. I will share more on how to achieve Delivery Mastery using systems and processes later.

Be Easy to Buy From

How easy have McDonald's made it to buy from them? You do not even need to get out of your car, and most times, you can point at a picture and grunt! Well, how easy is it to buy from you? Do customers have to fill in 6 pages of an application form and give you their inside leg measurements? Something as simple as giving online customers the option of a Guest Checkout instead of registering can make all the difference. Make sure you have credit card facilities or contactless pay. Think about how you can make it easier for people to give you their money.

CHAPTER 8

MASTERY SUMMARY

To move forwards, you need to make great decisions based on facts and figures. You need control. Without Mastery, the only thing holding a business up is the business owner's ability to run fast for a long time. You know that is not sustainable. You need foundations that will support your growth. Long term, one key individual cannot hold everything together. So, get to work on putting into place the things you read in Mastery, and you will feel much more control and a greater sense of confidence in moving your business forwards.

CHAPTER 9

GROWTH

I have given you a fundamental understanding of the basics of your business. Now you can move forwards safe in the knowledge that the growth of your business can be sustainable.

Price Competition

As mentioned before, price is an emotional topic. Even more emotive for me is people discounting to win work! People buy on price because you have given them nothing else to differentiate your product or service. So, they default to the lowest common denominator, price, when deciding who to buy from. Price competition is a blood bath, and you need to stay away from it. Remember, if your biggest competitor cuts their prices, your business model could fail. Competing on price does not give businesses a safe place to be in, and I do everything I can to get my clients away from it.

Guarantees

Would you go to the dentist who guaranteed no pain? Most people I know would! That dentist understands people's fear and guarantees against it. That is our job in business too. Understand your prospective customers' fears of doing business with you. Then put into place a

Growth

guarantee(s) that takes the fear or risk away from them, and makes it easier for them to try you out. When you have a USP or Guarantee that no one else does, you can charge whatever you like, therefore moving away from price competition.

We once coached a tiler whose three main clients were new home builders. Whenever these home builders had a new development, they would invite all the trades to submit their tenders. The trades would then try and get their prices as low as possible to win the work. When the winning bidders find out that they have been successful, the initial joy and euphoria would soon turn to frustration. The winners would have to do such a big job with such tight margins. It would typically be lots of headaches for no profit. Does this sound familiar? Well, it happens all around us every day.

So, we asked the tiler to survey his three clients. He asked, amongst other questions, *"What do you not like about tilers in general?"* Notice that he was asking about tilers in general, not just his company.

The home builders came back with three common themes in their answers:

1. 1You tilers are terrible at timekeeping, and your delays throw our building schedules out.

2. You tilers never clean up after yourselves. The house is always a mess when you finish. We must pay for another cleaner to come and tidy up your mess before we can complete the house.

3. You tilers can sometimes be careless when working and scuff a wall or scratch a door. We must pay to have it fixed before we can complete the house.

So, on the next set of tenders, we asked the tiler to put these bullet point guarantees on the front page:

- I GUARANTEE, if my team is late, you will get that job for FREE.
- I GUARANTEE, if my team leaves a mess, I will pay for the cleaner, and you will get that job for FREE.
- I GUARANTEE, if my team damage the property in any way, I will pay for it to be fixed, and you will get that job for FREE.

Simultaneously, we asked the tiler to increase his original price by 35%, more than he would have ever dreamt of quoting. As you can imagine, we encountered resistance from the tiler! To his credit, after many conversations, the tiler decided to do as we had asked. He submitted three tenders in an incredibly price-sensitive market. The tenders had the three bullet point guarantees with pricing 35% higher than he would have ever dreamt. He won two out of the three tenders he submitted.

If the price is the issue, then how was that possible? That proves price is not the issue. I know what most people reading this are saying, *"Well, Jas, you do not know my industry. It is different for us."* If only I had a pound for every time I had heard that!! In any purchasing decision at the exact moment the decision is made, there is 80% emotion and 20% logic. The emotion is usually fear, a fear of this new supplier letting the customer down. Our job is to understand that fear and to guarantee against it. For reference, the word *"guarantee"* is the second most powerful word in marketing after the word *"free."* So, what guarantees can you put in place that will reduce a first-time buyer's resistance and increase the trust they feel?

For those of you in regulated industries, you may have limitations to what you can guarantee. If so, you can have some fun! For example, I once coached a Solicitors firm, and they guaranteed that if the client yawned during their meeting, they would have to buy them lunch!

Years ago, during one of my seminars, a woman jumped up and exclaimed that she had spent £60k on a marketing company without any results. How was I any different? I replied, *"Did they give you any guarantees?"* To which she said, *"No."* I then replied, *"Well, I do!"* The woman sat down, and that was the end of that conversation. When you guarantee something, then people really cannot have a comeback.

Most people reading this will feel mortified by the prospect of offering a guarantee. *"It will bankrupt me, Jas!"* For my coaching clients, we build systems and processes in their business to deliver on the guarantee. Yet, if we fail to deliver on our guarantee, we should commit to doing what we said we would do. You should do 100% of the promise with no arguments.

This is about your integrity. So, compare the possible cost of a few guarantee claims against the potential new business you would get. If you know your numbers, you can calculate this.

USP

The Unique Selling Proposition (USP) is incredibly important. Some businesses just use this to take people away from price shopping. While it is not as powerful as a guarantee, it is still remarkably effective in protecting your margins from the discount seekers. It is essential to understand what a USP is. It is not, *"We give the best customer service"* or *"The best quality."* These statements are not unique as anyone could say that. How about, *"All our team goes through our unique 12 step training program which ensures that they give you the best possible service?"* You would create the 12-step program of course and it would be unique to your company.

The thing with creating USP's and guarantees is that your competition finds out. Soon, they will copy you, and your competitive advantage has gone. You will have to revert back to price competition. You have to keep innovating. A great example of the need for continual innovation is Apple. I have been using Apple as a great example of innovation for over a decade. Yet, at the time of writing this book in 2020, Apple, for the first time, is not the best example to use, but I am still going to use them!

If you buy Apple products, you know they are priced incredibly high when they first launch. Years

Growth

ago, Apple launched an MP3 player with a music purchasing system next to it, the iPod. As no one else offered this, they could charge what they wanted, a remarkably high price! If you look at the Innovation Curve below, you will see that the curve's left-hand side is innovation.

Once we go past the tipping point at the top of the curve, the product or service becomes a commodity, and the only differentiating factor is the price.

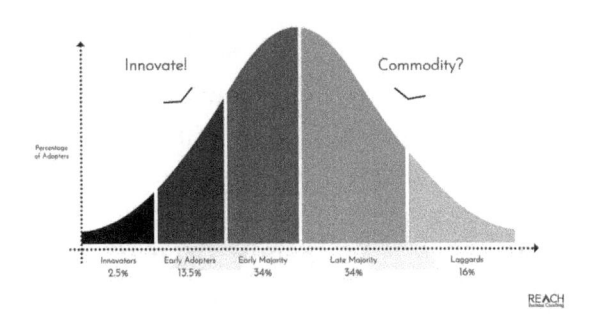

Innovate! — *Commodity?*

Percentage of Adopters

Innovators 2.5% | Early Adopters 13.5% | Early Majority 34% | Late Majority 34% | Laggards 16%

REACH

You can also find Appendix 13 at www.theeeplan.com

Apple realised this. After a few years, MP3 players were readily available, and the iPod became a commodity. That is why Apple continued to innovate and bring new products to the market, such as:

- The iPod Nano,
- The iPod Touch,
- The iPhone,
- The iPad,

- The Apple Watch,
- Air Pods

Every time they launched a new product, no one else could offer it. So, Apple could charge whatever they wanted to. I mentioned that Apple was not such a great example anymore because, for the first time, they are bringing products to the market that other companies have already created. So, how they fair with pricing when their products are not unique will be interesting to see.

With a bit of creativity, you can identify your possible USPs and your Guarantees. If you are not sure, ask your customers. They will tell you. If you have something different, that is what you tell people they are buying. That is why it is priced as it is. So, what can you do to differentiate yourself from your competition and protect your margin at the same time?

A-B-C-D Grading of Customers

There is a widely held myth that every customer is *"king."* Let me blow that out of the water right away: NO, THEY ARE NOT! What I want to do is to grade all your customers in 4 ways:

- "A" grade is the best of the best. They never haggle on price. They always pay on time and sometimes even in advance. They send you referrals. They write you testimonials. They are your raving fans. When you finish speaking to one of these customers, life is good!

- "B" grade does not haggle on price. Yet, occasionally they may be late paying, and they are not as forthcoming on referrals. They are good reliable customers, though.
- "C" grade haggles on price most of the time, and most of the time, they pay late.
- "D" grade is the worst of the worst. They always haggle on price. They are your worst payers. They throw in a fictitious complaint to delay paying their invoice. They will only speak to the "boss." They bad mouth you to other people. Often, they leave you or your team in tears. You are probably feeling sick in the pit of your stomach, thinking of your "D" grade clients right now.

Here is how I go about helping my clients grade their clients. I ask my clients to rank their clients on a scale of 1 to 5 in 5 key categories. 1 being poor and 5 being excellent. The five key categories are:

1. How profitable on average is each transaction?
2. How much turnover do they give us per annum?
3. How many referrals do they send us?
4. How quickly do they pay?
5. How much do they adhere to our values?

I believe it is essential to use a wide range of variables. Because your best customer for turnover might still be the worst payer and least aligned to your values, you must use a wide range of factors to measure this.

Once you have this data in a spreadsheet, you can tally up the scores for all five categories and decide how to define *"A," "B," "C,"* and *"D."* For example:

17-20 = *"A"* grade

13-16 = *"B"* grade

8-12 = *"C"* grade

<7 = *"D"* grade

The above scale is just an example. You will decide on your way to do this.

So, once you have graded them, what do you do with the clients? I will show you that you do not need your *"D"* grade clients. Every transaction with these *"energy vampires"* you do is at a loss. You must factor in the cost of your time in the full cost of making that sale. Remember *"D"* clients only want to speak to you. What about the other intangible costs? For example, the dark cloud that descends on your day when you know you must talk to a *"D"* grade. Consider the atmosphere it leaves in your team that day when one of them has been reduced to tears by a *"D"* grade.

You do not need your *"D"* grade clients. If you *"sack"* them, will you lose sales? Yes, of course, you will. But, what will happen to your profit? It will soar! In one example, I increased a client's profit by over 800% by getting them to stop working with *"D"* grade clients. Remember, you cannot measure the emotional impacts of not having to have your day spoiled by these people.

Growth

I believe that emotional, intangible costs are much greater than tangible costs.

This is also an ideal time to use our values to help you make these tough decisions; we mentioned this earlier in the Values section. You inform the *"D"* grade clients that due to their inability to adhere to your company values, with regret, you cannot continue to do business with them. Please keep this communication professional and above the line. PS, the best way to get rid of *"D"* grade clients is to keep putting their price up!

You can upgrade some *"C"* grade clients to a *"B"* or even an *"A"* with some simple communication that repositions how you will want to work going forwards. For example: *"Dear Bob, going forwards, this is how we want to work with all our customers (proceed to list how you want this to look, remembering to use your values). If you agree with this, we would love to continue our relationship. If not, here is a list of possible other suppliers you may want to consider."*

So, let us go back to the *"A"* and *"B"* grade clients. We usually find that 80% of our business comes from 20% of our clients, the *"A"* and *"B"* grades. Do you think this 20% of clients get 80% of your time? Do they even get 20% of your time? No. This 20% of your clients who are responsible for 80% of your business are lucky to get even 5% of your time because you spend 95% of your time dealing with *"D"* grade clients. *"D"* grade clients who lose you money!!! This phenomenon is insane, and I hope many of you are having light bulb moments galore right now!

What would happen if these "A" and "B" grade clients got more of your time, care, and attention? Is it possible that they may send you even more business? Yes, because they already really like you! So, what are you going to do with these clients?

For the "A" grade clients, you need to do so much more. Make them your VIPs as people love this. What could that mean for them? Do they get a dedicated Account Manager? Does your telephone system recognise their number when they call you? Do they immediately go to the top of the call queue? Do you give their orders priority shipping? Do you go out and see them every quarter? Do you send them a birthday card and a Wedding Anniversary card? Do you even create a VIP card? The list is endless, but this is something you can go to town on because these people deserve it.

For the "B" grade clients, I recommend monthly or worst-case quarterly telephone care calls. Use these personal calls to check in on them to see if everything is okay and show them you care about them.

Imagine how much more enjoyable life would be without your "D" grade clients? And remember, all these calculations fail to consider the intangible costs of doing business with "D" grades. Imagine how your team would respond if you told them that you were no longer working with these clients because they had been rude and abusive to them, and their behaviour was not in line with our values? Is it possible that the emotional bank balance has a massive deposit to you from your team?

Growth

Years ago, I coached a company with one client responsible for over 60% of their turnover. Dealing with this client was horrible. They would regularly leave my client in tears with their *"bully boy"* tactics. One day, my client had had enough. They sacked the client! Losing over 60% of your annual turnover in one day will have a severe impact on your business. There were days in the following months when we were unsure if we would make it, but we came through with hard work and intense focus. Today, the business has a much healthier spread of clients. No one client is responsible for any more than 10% of company turnover. My client and their team are the happiest, most content, and the most productive they have ever been. How long can you afford not to deal with this?

Every time you say *"yes"* to a *"D"* grade client, you are saying *"no"* to an *"A"* grade client. You are also sending a clear message to the universe, *"Please send me any type of customer, I will take anyone."* So, what are you going to do to stop working with loss-making, energy-sapping clients so that you can spend more time with the clients that you want to?

Test and Measure

There is an old saying that *"50% of marketing works, we just don't know which 50%!"* Too often, I see businesses throwing money away on marketing strategies that do not work. How then, do we know which 50% of marketing works? We must ask one critical question from this day forward when someone we do not know gets in touch, *"Can I please ask where you heard about us from?"*

Years ago, I coached a client who spent £1500 per month on a specific advert in their industry's most prominent magazine. They had been running this advert for over seven years when I began working with them. I began by asking everyone handling sales enquiries to start asking the golden question whenever someone got in touch that was not already on our database. *"Can I ask, where did you hear about us from?"* After six weeks, we analysed the results. Guess how many enquiries came from this £1500 per month advert? I will give you a clue – it is a big fat round number! Yes, this advert, which may have worked over seven years ago, was generating zero enquiries! By pulling the advert, we immediately saved the client £18k per year. We discovered that Google search yielded over 90% of queries. So, what we did was divert some of these resources into SEO.

Another example from many years ago was where a client always spent more than £12k per year on Yellow Pages advertising. Yes, it was many years ago! When we started asking the golden question, we found that the *"A-Boards"* outside on the main road generated all the new enquiries. Immediately we stopped the Yellow Pages adverts and made the *"A-Boards"* bigger!

We tested and measured so that we could make sound decisions. Where should this test and measure information be stored? Yes, the Dashboard!

Remember, the golden question is, *"Can I please ask where you heard about us from?"* What do you need to do to put the golden question into your process so that your team ask it every time someone new contacts you?

CHAPTER 10

FIVE WAYS TO GROW YOUR BUSINESS

Most people I first come across tell me that they want more customers, more turnover, and more profit. In the diagram below (You can also see the diagram in Appendix 14 at www.theeeplan.com), you will see that these 3 things cannot be directly influenced as they have equals signs before them, they are outputs.

REACH's 5 Ways to Increase Your Business Profits...

Number of Leads
×
Conversion Rate
=
No. of Customers
×
No. of Transactions
×
Ave. £££ Sale
=
Revenues
×
Margin
=
Profits

We can however, influence the other five things, hence we call this *"The 5 Ways."*

1. **Leads** – How many qualified enquiries can you attract?

2. **Conversion Rate** – How many of these enquiries can you convert to paying customers?

Five Ways to Grow Your Business

3. **Average Value Sale** – On average, how much do people spend?

4. **Number of Transactions** – On average, how often do people come back to buy from you over any given time period, like a year, for example?

5. **Margins** – On average, what is the profit margin per transaction?

One of the widely held myths in business is that the only way you can grow is to bring in new customers. If you are a brand-new business, then yes, this is the only way you can grow. For everyone else, I hope I can prove in this chapter that there is massive potential sitting in your business in the four other areas:

1. Conversion Rate
2. Average Value Sale
3. Number of Transactions
4. Margins

Typically, these four areas do not cost much or anything at all to grow. Generating leads does cost most of the time. These 4 areas could make you hundreds of thousands of pounds in turnover and profits for little or no cost. When working through the 5 Ways with a client, I usually do things in this order:

1. Margins
2. Conversion Rate

3. Average Value Sale

4. Number of Transactions

5. Leads

Doing Leads first with a client would be like trying to fill the bath with the plug out. When we bring in new leads, we want them to generate a profit. To have the best chance of new leads generating a profit, you must have a handle on the other four areas first. In this chapter, I will share strategies in each area that will give you the quickest return on investment. For the purposes of this chapter, I will go through each of the 5 Ways in the order they are in the diagram.

Leads

How do you get prospects beating a path to your door? There are lots of different ways to drive new enquiries to your business. I will discuss some of the most important and cost-effective.

1. Target Market

2. Direct Mail

3. Secret Salesforce

4. Strategic Alliance

Target Market

Who is your target market? Too often, business owners engage in scattergun marketing where they are firing as many pellets out of their gun, hoping that one might hit a target. This type of marketing is costly and not the best use of your time. You need to define who your target market(s) are and target them specifically. Do not start looking for new enquiries until you have defined your target market. One client of mine was a high-end furniture retailer. Before working with me, the business spent over £500k per annum on marketing. This marketing was to the masses with no specific targeting. We do not fully know how successful the results were because there was no test and measure in place. Upon seeing these numbers, I asked my client to start segmenting their customers. We found that they fitted into two distinct categories.

1. Mid-40s, young family, professionals, high disposable income.

2. Mid-60s, retired, stay at home.

Armed with this information, we asked the marketing company we were using to precisely craft a message aimed at these two groups. As you can imagine, the language you would use for one group would be different than that used for the other, hence we needed a different message for each segment. This action alone saved £100k per annum on marketing because we did not spend so much money talking to everyone. We just focused on these two groups with who we knew we wanted to do business. Some of you may be thinking, *"aren't we going to miss out on lots of other customers?"* Yes, possibly, but, to put your mind at rest, once we focused on just these two specific target markets, we achieved our record profit margin in the business's 75-year history because the people targeted were the ones that we made the most profit from.

Another example of targeted marketing comes from a small marketing agency. The agency had been making the mistake of scattergun marketing. Even marketing companies make this mistake. Specifically, there was an engineering company that the marketing company had wanted to work with for years. The marketing company continued wasting time and money, sending them generic marketing. Indeed, they could not even get past the gatekeeper when trying to speak to the MD of the engineering company.

After understanding the importance of the *"target market,"* the marketing company began researching the engineering company. They found that the company manufactured motor engines and that their first engine had run in a car in the prestigious Le Mans 24-hour motor race. Now, it just so happened that the marketing company owner had been attending the Le Mans 24-hour race every year for as long as he could remember. So, we went about writing a letter specifically to the engineering company. Down the letter's left-hand side, we drew a timeline highlighting where the car running with their engine had finished in the race. Down the right-hand side of the letter, we drew a timeline highlighting where the marketing company owner had been in his life when attending the race. For example, *"got married"* and *"had a first child,"* etc. The letter body was a couple of handwritten (yes handwritten) paragraphs just introducing the marketing agency. We also sourced a toy model version of the car that

Five Ways to Grow Your Business

the engine had been in on the first-ever race and sent it to the engineering company. The very next day, the head of the engineering company called the marketing company, asking for their help. Remember, the marketing company had been trying for years to *"open the door"* with this engineering company, but the moment they became more targeted, then bingo! So, who is your target market (be specific), and how will you talk to them?

Direct Mail

A personal favourite of mine is direct mail. People say that direct mail does not work. Let me tell you, yes, it does! Over the last decade (2010-2020), more and more people have ditched *"snail mail"* for online approaches instead. A significant belief of mine has been that when everyone else *"zigs,"* you need to *"zag."* That is why I passionately believe that you need to send direct mail. A recent report said that some 16-year-olds have never received a letter in their lives. When was the last time you received something in the post other than a bill? No matter what happens with trends, especially with technology, we remain the same basic animals. 80% of the population are visual and kinaesthetic, which means they respond better to sight and, more importantly, touch.

Another primary reason why direct mail does not work is that marketers do it in the same boring way. White envelope with a window with the recipient details typed, normally postage franked. This kind of mail stands out like junk mail and invariably ends up in the bin. We need to be different, and the way we do it is by following the teachings of Jay Conrad Levinson, the founder and God Father of *"Guerrilla Marketing."*

1. Bright coloured envelope such as green, red, or yellow. The brighter, the better.

2. Handwritten name and address.

3. Many stamps. If, for example, the price of a postage stamp is 60, then put on a 50, 5, 2, 2, 1.

4. Put a gimmick in the envelope with the letter, something that will stick out to create curiosity. That is why I call this strategy "lumpy mail."

The copy of the letter is important, and you can find some examples in Appendix 15 at www.theeeplan.com. Include some fundamental things like a photo of you; the headline must link back to the gimmick in the envelope, an offer, a call to action, and a PS. All these things will improve your chances of getting a positive result. Yet, what will make the most significant difference to this campaign is the follow-up phone call. Simply sending some *"lumpy mail"* will result in a 0.01% response rate. Calling them up after they receive the letter will result in a 5% response rate. The swing is massive!

The follow-up phone call needs to be structured to ensure it gives you the best possible opportunity to get you to the next stage. You are not looking for a sale

Five Ways to Grow Your Business

right now. You are looking to move the prospect to the next stage of your sales process. The biggest mistake people make when conducting any type of sales calls, such as face to face, email, or phone, is that they go to sales mode far too quickly. The sales process I teach comes from a great book by Duane Sparks called *"Action Selling."* In the book, Sparks talks about sales being like a play in the Theatre. If the Theatre gets the Acts in the wrong sequence, then the end of the theatrical production does not make sense. The same is true in sales. You see, many people complain that they just cannot get people over the line at the end of the process. I promise you that if you struggle to get people over the line at the end of your sales process, your issue is much further back. You see, if you do the steps of your sales process correctly, then closing becomes the easiest part, not the most challenging part.

The best advice I can give you is to slow down and ask great questions to understand the prospect's needs. And only when you have exhausted this process do you dare to present your proposal. Most salespeople jump into proposal mode way too early before understanding their prospect's needs.

Going back to the direct mail, the gimmick in this process is especially important. With respect to you, nine times out of 10, your letter will go in the bin. What they will remember when you call is the gimmick you sent. Now, a gimmick is not a diary or a pen. That will not get remembered! It must be something that everyone in the office remembers. And when you call in following up, you will have a joke with the gatekeeper, and while you are on good terms, you will ask to be put through to the prospect. I have a list of gimmicks (lumps), and you can find them in Appendix 16 at www.theeeplan.com.

The best strategy we ever used in our business was a 2-step direct mail process. We used the technique to attract more Accountants and Solicitors to do our flagship Cycle of Business Success Workshops with. We sent a letter, and the gimmick was a disposable wooden fork. The PS told them to *"keep the fork as they would need it."* The very next day, a courier delivered a sponge cake. Without a doubt, this strategy has given us the best return on investment ever because who does not like cake?!

So, how can you get creative and start using direct mail to your advantage?

Secret Salesforce

We have an active sales force under our noses who will sell for us once we have asked them and trained them. We must teach our clients about the type of referrals we want and how they can refer people to us. We must also remind our clients about referrals regularly. Most people have millions of messages thrown at them every day. No matter how much they love you, your clients will forget about you and miss out on sending you potential *"A"* grade referrals. My practice is to remind my clients twice every 13 weeks.

Years ago, I coached a software reselling company. They had particularly challenging targets to meet for

Five Ways to Grow Your Business

new sales every year from the software company. The number of new sales they needed to do every year was 225. The software company had a no-nonsense commission scheme for all of their resellers, which meant that if we hit 225 new sales and beyond, then the higher rate of commission was paid on all sales. Even if we fell short by one sale (224), we would receive a lower commission rate on all sales. The difference in commission payments between 224 and 225 sales a year was more than £100,000.

In early November, we calculated that we would hit precisely 225 new sales by year-end. But the risk was that people had a 30-day cooling-off period. Meaning we could be sitting on 225 new sales on New Year's Eve toasting our success, and just one client could cancel. That solitary cancellation would cost the company over £100,000 in commissions. A risk too big; I hope you will all agree!

So, we put a basic email together, asking the existing clients if they knew anyone interested in buying their software. If the referral did indeed buy a new licence, then the current client (the referrer) would receive one of 3 different gifts. None of the gifts cost us more than £100 to buy. The other number to remember was that there were more than £3,000 profit in each new sale of the software.

We sent that email in the first week of November, and before the end of November, we had signed eight new clients! These eight new clients would give us more than enough of a buffer zone to ensure we hit and exceeded the 225 new licences target. Now, for a cost to us of no more than £800 (the gifts to the referrer), we made more than £24,000 in profit. Who would not invest £800 to make more than £24,000?! Bigger than that of course was that the £800 investment had ensured we made the extra £100k in sales commissions!

It is important only to ask your *"A"* and *"B"* grade clients for referrals. If you ask *"C"* and *"D"* grade clients, what are they more than likely to send you? Yes, more *"C"* and *"D's!"* Even more reason for doing the *"ABCD"* grading exercise!

What referral system are you going to design, and how will you remind your *"A"* and *"B"* grade clients about it regularly?

Strategic Alliances

Without a doubt, my absolute favourite lead generation strategy is strategic alliances. Who do you know that is not in competition with you but has the same types of target market customers, and how could you form a mutually beneficial relationship?

For example, let us say I own a ladies-hairdressing salon and am after some new customers. I notice that Angela runs a ladies-beauty salon down the road, and she has the types of clients that I want. I approach Angela with a letter that I have written that I want her to send to her clients. The letter looks like Angela wrote it and gives thanks to her customers for their continued loyal support. The letter says, *"By way of thanking you, I have arranged for you to get a free haircut*

Five Ways to Grow Your Business

normally costing £60." All her customers must do is bring the letter to my salon to get their free haircut.

I am going to charge Angela nothing for doing this. I will even pay for the envelopes and stamps. All she must do is put her customer's details on the letter and post them as that is her data we are using.

When her customers receive this letter, might Angela's *"emotional bank balance"* have a significant deposit? Yes, absolutely! When people get something nice, they tend to show off to other people about it, so Angela will also get some free marketing.

So, what will it cost me to do these free haircuts? Well, because I have Money Mastery, I know that the actual costs are £25 to do a haircut. Yet, when Angela's customers visit my hairdressing salon, remember, they must bring the letter with them that has their details on it. We will put those details onto our system, market to them forever, and blow them away with our excellent customer service. We could also possibly even give them a special offer for their 2nd visit. So, while we are *"losing"* £25 on the first visit, I know that my customers come back every six weeks on average. On average, my customers stay with me for 11 years. So, I have invested £25 to make over £3,300 in profit. That is calculated by £35 profit per visit multiplied by a repeat visit every six weeks for 11 years. Not a bad return, hey? Would you invest £25 to make £3,300???

Another example of this would be a pet food store and dog kennels. They are after the same target market but not in competition. How could these two businesses form a mutually beneficial relationship?

An old client of mine has a farm shop and tea rooms. They wanted more clients. They approached a local hairdressing salon and asked if they could leave an A5 postcard type flyer in the salon. It would give the salon customers a free cup of tea and a slice of cake if they brought in the flyer. Of course, they had to complete the other side of the flyer with their details! The great thing we found here was that even on the first visit, the salon customers were buying stuff from the shop as they had to walk through the shop to get to the team rooms! We earned a profit from the first visit, which is as good as it gets. At the last count, that A5 flyer resulted in over 600 new customers at the farm shop and counting!

Too many people think tactically instead of strategically. Do not look for 100 new customers. Start looking for the business that already has those 100 customers and would be happy to introduce you.

So, who do you know that you could partner with to create a mutually beneficial relationship?

Conversion Rate

Of the Five Ways, the conversion rate is my favourite. I love this one because it has such incredible power to transform a business. Whatever you increase the conversion rate by, you increase the business by the same amount. I come across many business owners who can be quite dismissive of this area, thinking they

Five Ways to Grow Your Business

have this one under control. Then we measure it, and instead of the boasted *"90% conversion rate,"* it comes out nearer 12%! I console these business owners with one powerful fact – we could not have done much if your conversion rate were 90%, but we sure can do a lot with 12%! Remember, if we get it to 24% in this example, we have doubled the business!!

The best way to increase your conversion rate is to start measuring it. Remember, you cannot manage what you do not measure! Also, by shining a light on this area, you create energy, attention, and focus. All this conspires to increase the conversion rate.

Sales Process

As mentioned previously, when talking about direct mail, sales is a process. Members of the sales force must follow each step of this process in a specific sequence. Then the close will be the easiest part, not the most challenging part of the process. In his brilliant book *"Action Selling,"* Sparks also talks about how most salespeople go for the pitch far too soon. They are so excited by how their great product or service will change the prospect's life if they buy it, that they don't bother even asking what the prospect's needs are.

Instead, the better way of approaching sales is in this order:

1. Introduce yourself. This builds rapport.

2. Introduce your business. This builds credibility.

3. Ask the best questions. This builds trust.

4. Make any proposals.

It sounds simple and obvious. Well, how many people do it this way? How many people instead do not bother building up any rapport or credibility?

Any good sales process should be jammed full of great open-ended questions that go deep and create emotion. 80% of sales decisions are made emotionally, and then the remaining 20% is the rational justification for the decision. Every business, therefore, should craft approximately 6 *"killer questions."* Questions that anyone at any stage of the sales process can ask to begin understanding the prospect better. Whoever asks the best questions will get the sale!

Two Ears, One Mouth

As a society, we are sick of salespeople telling us what they think we need. How many of you woke up one Saturday morning and turned round to your family and said, *"Let's go to the shop to be sold a new TV today?!"* Our job in business is to help people to buy. The best equipment a salesperson can buy is a notebook and a pen. Then ask great questions, give the nod to whatever they say, and take copious amounts of notes. When we go to the Doctor's surgery, what does the Doctor do? They ask lots of questions, take lots of notes, and nod. At the end, when they suggest their solution, do we reject their prescription? At the sales meeting, only after they answer all your questions, do you even begin to talk about your solution to the prospect. When you do, you tie certain aspects back to what they said earlier during the questioning. For example, *"I recommend a red one because you said red was your favourite colour."* My entire philosophy on sales is tied into this next statement, *"At the end of any sales interaction, it is more important for the prospect to know that you have understood their needs than it is for them to even know what you sell."* If you embrace this principle, you will understand why asking the best questions is the most crucial part of sales.

The other thing that a sales process does is iron out massively fluctuating conversion rates within your existing team. If you have more than one person selling in your business, you will probably know what I am talking about! Having one person convert at 60% and another at 17% is frustrating and extremely hard to forecast. A documented sales process reduces variation in conversion rate to +/- 5% if followed by everyone. In our business, anyone can follow our fully documented sales process, and we can accurately forecast a conversion rate variation of even less than +/- 5% regardless of who is following it.

Number of Transactions

It is six times cheaper to get your old customers to buy from you again than it is to go out and buy new customers. If that is the case, should we not be spending more time nurturing existing customer relationships? The sad fact is that most businesses would rather keep pouring water into a bucket to keep topping it up instead of trying to fix the leak at the bottom! Continuously pouring water into a leaky bucket is what we do when we lack focus on enhancing existing relationships and getting old clients to come back. Studies have proven that 68% of customers will stop buying from a business because of *"perceived indifference."* It does not matter how much you think they love you. If you do not show enough care and attention to your customers, one day, they will go elsewhere because they believe you are taking them for granted. And that is the real kick in the guts! If that happens to you, you deserve it because you did not care enough about them. No doubt, most of your time would have been spent dealing with *"D"* grade clients who lose you money! I hope this realisation makes you even more determined to sack those *"D"* grade clients and start focusing more on the *"A"* and *"B"* grades.

You must do more to keep in touch with your existing customers. Merely assuming that sending them an invoice keeps you in touch with them is flawed thinking. How do you continue to add value?

My preferred method of adding value to an existing customer relationship is a Blog/Newsletter. A Blog/Newsletter allows you to stay in touch with customers, but at the same time adding value. A note of warning; article content with more than 15% selling goes in the bin or gets deleted. Do not sell; add value.

A car salesman in the US uses this principle to significant effect in his business. Rough estimates say that the average repeat buying cycle for a new car in the US is approximately four years. When you buy a car from this dealership, you receive a postcard from

Five Ways to Grow Your Business

them every single month. The postcard reminds the customer that if there are any problems with the car, then they should not hesitate to bring it straight back to the dealer, and they will fix it. Who do you think stays *"front of mind"* for those four years? And when the next buying decision is due to be made, for example, in 3 years and 11 months, who do you think will at least get the chance to pitch for the new sale? For a cost of 48 stamps and 48 postcards, that business will get the opportunity of a $50,000 deal. If you stay in front of the mind of your customer, yours will be the name they think of first when the next buying decision needs making.

Please do not fall foul of the assumption that *"they know we are here, and if they want something, they will get in touch."* This flawed assumption costs businesses millions of pounds in lost sales every year. Get on the front foot and stay in touch!

So how will you stay front of mind to ensure you get the chance to make the next sale the customer wants to make?

Average Value Sale

Do you want fries with that? Did you know that at one point, that question made McDonald's over £50m a day in global sales? More importantly, did you know that 30% of people that said *"yes"* to *"do you want fries with that?"* had no intention of buying fries when originally placing their order? Even more importantly, did you know that the same 30% ratio applies to every business on earth, even yours? If you had your own *"do you want fries with that"* questions, 30% of customers would say *"yes!"* So, it makes sense to create these questions and ensure that they are asked by everyone on every sale. And that is where many people fall short. If a few people ask the question, it will make some difference, but if everyone asks it, every time, it will make a massive difference. Please take the time to train the team, role play, quizzes; I do not care how. Train, train, train!

You do not even need to sell the product or service you are offering to the customer. Years ago, I coached a garage. Sometimes when servicing a car, they noticed some bodywork damage. They would mention to the car owner that they should take their car to the body shop down the road. If they did, the body shop would give the garage a *"finders-fee."* Likewise, if the body shop were repairing a damaged car and noticed that the service light was on, they would recommend the garage to the car owner and be rewarded by the garage.

What are your *"do you want fries with that"* questions, and how can we build them into every transaction?

Profit Margins

You are in business for profit! Everything you do must manifest itself here. While all 4 of the previous Five Ways will work their way down to here, you can still do so much more in this area. Most important here is pricing, which I already covered in Money Mastery.

Another area is the costs. I often see a P&L where lots of payments are still going out for things you no

Five Ways to Grow Your Business

longer use. The look of bewilderment on the business owner's face when they see these costs is only matched by the astonishment on my face when I realise that they did not know that they still made the payments! When was the last time you went down all your costs line by line? When was the last time you tried to get a better deal from your suppliers? Why not set yourself a target to reduce your costs by a certain percentage? That will focus the mind. Cutting costs will increase profit margins the same as growing sales. While all successful people make their fortunes growing sales, all the people who have fortunes are laser-like in their attention to the costs too.

5 Ways Summary

Are you familiar with the concept of marginal gains? Marginal gains are where you make minor improvements across many areas to achieve a considerable impact. Well, earning a substantial profit is what happens when you work all the Five Ways. Look at this table in Appendix 17 at www.theeeplan.com if you do not believe me. There are no *"smoke and mirrors"* here. If you achieved a 10% increase across all of the Five Ways, this is what would happen. If you work in percentages, then in this example, that is a 46% increase in turnover and a 61% increase in profit! Who thinks this would be a good thing to do in their business?

Now, in some businesses, you cannot make a 10% increase in some areas. For example, a high-end kitchen manufacturer will struggle to increase the number of transactions in the same year when most people will have that kitchen for many years. If you are one of those businesses, please remember that we are referring to an average 10% increase across all the Five Ways in this example. If you cannot increase one area, try to increase the other four by another 2.5%. Whatever premutation, you want to achieve an average of 10% across all of the Five Ways.

Most business owners are oblivious to this formula. They spend their entire lives thinking the only way to improve their businesses is to get more leads. Well, I hope I have shown you that in every business, except a brand new one, there is stacks of potential in 4 other areas you can extract for little or no cost before you need to bring in new leads. I have spent three years coaching one client on the four different areas of the Five Ways. We still have not even looked at Lead Generation because we are too busy making money in the other four areas!!

Now you have the secret to growing your business. Most times, you can grow without spending a penny on marketing. It is time to get to work!

So, which one of the Five Ways will you begin working on first?

CHAPTER 11

GROWTH SUMMARY

I did not aim to write this book to be just about marketing. Yet, I hope that this section has given you more than enough to think about to increase your profitability. At least it should get you started on marketing in a structured and organised manner. As always, there is a direct correlation between how much quality time you give to something and the results you get from it. Let's get to work on growing the business.

CHAPTER 12

LEVERAGE

Here is where we are going to start making the business scale. Remember, systems run the business; people run the systems; you lead the people.

The most successful business owners understand leverage. They know that the overriding theme of leverage is, do the work once, get paid back forever. You see, if you have been kind enough to buy this book, then I will have hopefully been paid for it. I only wrote the book once, but I am getting paid for it every time some beautiful soul purchases it. I want you to take that exact principle into your business every single day from now on. How can you do something once and get paid back forever?

- Without systems, you cannot achieve leverage.
- Without systems, you cannot leave your business.
- Without systems, you must always work hard.

I do not know about you, but I do not like hard work! Remember, think lazy.

When it comes to getting systems to do the work, I like to go through a 3-step process to achieve leverage.

Process Flows

Get everyone in the team away from the business for an entire day. Ideally, hire a large hotel meeting room/boardroom. The room needs to have at least one big wall that you can use. Get lots of post-it-notes and pens; you are going to need them! The aim is to plot what happens in the business through the entire customer journey.

Starting on the left-hand side of the wall, begin using post-it-notes to plot what happens in the business from start to finish. Let us say we start with marketing. We use a post-it-note for each type of marketing activity. Off each marketing activity post-it-note, there needs to be a new post-it-note for each thing that could happen from that marketing activity. For example, a marketing activity post-it-note could be *"Website Enquiry."* Off this post-it-note would be another post-it-note called *"Submits Website Contact Form."* Then, get another post-it-note for what happens next when the website contact form is submitted. Keep going through the entire operation like this.

Getting the team involved with healthy discussions on how the process should flow leads to process improvement. For example, you may encounter a particularly bad point where you seem to get lots of customer complaints. You can discuss this to see how you can improve it by adding/subtracting/amending processes around this *"pain point."*

You can move post-it-notes. Some people in the team may disagree where things currently go, so it is good to move the post-it-notes around. You should have the business mapped out in the way that you all agree it should be. Please be reassured that I hold no interest in any companies who make post-it-notes!

You may need more than one day. You may need to spend an entire day on each functional area of your business. Please record in writing the agreed-upon process flows and take photos of the wall at the end of each session.

Once you have your ideal process flow mapped out, go to work on making them into a professional document. You can either do it yourself or, if like me; you are not a ninja at creating process maps, you can outsource it. I recommend www.fiverr.com, as I have used them many times. Simply search for *"process flows."* You will see a list of people worldwide who will turn your scrap pieces of paper or photos into professional process flow maps.

These nicely created documents allow you to regularly take a step back from your business and assess your processes. Remember, when something breaks, always look for a systems solution, not a people solution. For example, if someone forgot to send a client an email giving directions to our office for a meeting, then add it to the process for New Client Meetings. If we think we can rely on people remembering to do things, we are destined to suffer failures in our business.

Can you imagine blowing these process maps up into large boards and having them displayed in the workplace? Could this drive more discussions around

Leverage

systems solutions? An old client of mine was in web design. Their sales process involved the prospect coming into their offices for meetings. Upon arriving at their offices, prospects saw the entire operation in the form of a process map on the meeting room wall. Can you imagine the reassurance people get when seeing this? Even at a subconscious level, I am sure that this improves people's perception of you as trustworthy, professional, and reliable. I cannot say with 100% certainty that the visibility of the process map on the wall directly affected the conversion rate in this business. Still, it cannot be a coincidence that after we displayed it, our conversion rate increased by nearly 30%!!!

How-To Manuals

Process mapping the entire business also tells you which *"how-to"* manuals you need to write. Each one of those processes on those post-it-notes needs a detailed document showing how to do it. And when I say detailed, I mean detailed! The over-riding principle of leverage is *"do the work once, get paid back forever."* Once you have created the *"how-to"*, people must be able to follow it without having to ask you questions. If they must come to you because the *"how-to"* is not clear or ambiguous, it has not worked. When I say detailed, I mean down to the keystroke level. One client even pasted a photo of a computer with an arrow pointing to the power button and wrote, *"Press this button to turn the computer on!"* You might say that this was a bit extreme, but you cannot be too detailed in my view.

One note of caution here is that only detailed people should write the *"how-to"* manuals. If you give this task to someone whose behavioural profile is not detailed, you will end up with a sketchy *"how-to"* document that people cannot follow.

From today onwards, every single week, I want you to target yourself to capture one routine daily task that you carry out in your business. It could be how you process the payroll, how you send invoices, how you pay the window cleaner; I don't care, but what you have to do is get it out of your head. If you keep it in your head, you are destined to do it forever.

The aim is to create a *"how-to"* manual for the business. Write a detailed step by step process guide for how you run the business. I want you to think like you are a franchise. You may have no intention of ever being a franchise, but please bear with me. Imagine you had 80 franchisees. Could you go round each of those 80 every morning to show them how to open up the shop? Of course not! You would rely on a manual. That is precisely the manual you are going to create for your business.

The *"how-to"* does not just have to be a written document. You must also consider other media like photos and videos. Indeed, from an interaction perspective, these are much more able to be processed and understood by the intended recipient. The bonus is that photos and videos are much quicker to create than a written document.

Leverage

When it comes to saving time, and improving the user experience, the *"Daddy"* of *"how-to"* manuals is screen recordings. Screen recordings have revolutionised how people create *"how-to"* manuals, and for me, nothing beats it. Best of all, it is free! If you are a Mac user, you will find the facility in QuickTime Player, and if you are a Windows user, then it is hidden in the Xbox app. (This is true at the time of writing this book.) If it changes, just Google it. If Microsoft and Apple decide to remove this free tool from their software, then you will have to pay for some software to do this for you. The cost of the software is relatively cheap. Whatever the cost may be, it will be far outweighed by the savings in your time by creating the *"how-to"* manual and not having to do that task again.

Recently a client had set time aside to document *"how-to"* manuals in his business. It was invoicing clients, which in his own words, *"was a pain in the neck because I have always been the only one who knew how to do it."* He set himself an hour to document this process and, at the last minute, decided to screen record how to invoice instead. In astonishment, he reported back to me that the entire process had taken 90 seconds to record!!! Remember, you are already carrying out most of these tasks. All you need to do is to press the record button and talk through what you do, and voila, the completed system will pay you back forever when you delegate it to someone else to do. Remember to slow down when you do the recording. Although you can do this process with your eyes shut, the person watching the recording will need more time to get it into their heads!

In our different businesses, we rely on outsourced workers in other parts of the world to help us. We have two people in the Philippines who have been with us for several years who we view as our team members. I supplement my requests for new workpieces and the work they do regularly with detailed *"how-to"* videos. The new work request with the *"how-to"* video works perfectly every time and has not let us down yet. Recording, writing, photographing the system only needs to happen once, but it saves your time forever!

One system in my Business Coaching business is preparing for my coaching weeks. The preparation usually takes me 5 hours per week to do. Screen recording how to do it took me approximately 30 minutes. I sent it to one of my team in the Philippines, and without one question, they did all my preparation for the following week without one error. The screen recording earned me a significant return on investment on my time, and will save me time every future week forever.

The vision is to create an entire library of *"how-to"* manuals. Can you imagine an Index page where every functional area of your business is a heading, and then underneath each heading are all the *"how-to"* manuals? Even sexier, can you imagine your business process map as an electronic document? The hyperlinks take

Leverage

the user to the relevant *"how-to"* manual. Are you getting excited? You should be because this will change your business and give you your life back! Best of all, this does not cost a penny to do. You can start doing it right now, even if you have not done the process mapping yet!

Some of you reading this book will wonder how you can document things when everything you do is bespoke. Over the years, I have coached many creative and design businesses who have wondered the same thing. Let me tell you how to deal with this challenge with a story. In 2009, I played football or *"soccer"* to my North American friends reading this. Unfortunately, I suffered a severe knee injury that required many operations. Angela kept telling me my playing days were over well before this injury! During one of these operations, I received an epidural and was mildly sedated. I recall watching the surgeon staring at a large TV screen, recording the camera in my knee. The surgeon was also wearing a hands-free headset into which he was speaking. He later explained to me that he lectured at the university, and he had wanted to capture my injury as a case study to use with his students. I suppose I should be flattered! It is the principle of case studies that I want to share with you, especially if your business does bespoke work.

Starting today, begin recording a project from start to finish: all the meetings, the designs, the drawings, the emails, absolutely everything. Get out of your head your thought processes as you proceed through that project. Imagine having a library of case studies for your team members to watch and use for training. Even better, imagine giving these case studies to a new team member before they even start. They can become inducted into your way of working in their time, not yours. Whatever you decide to do, these recordings will pay you back forever, but you only create them once.

An ex-client of mine was a builder. He said he couldn't document the thought processes he went through when approaching a derelict building for the first time. As he said, *"That is just 30 years of experience."* So, I told him that the next time he approached a new job for the first time and every subsequent time, take out your mobile phone and start recording a video while walking the site, talking your thoughts. Again, this library of case studies you create will have millions of pounds worth of value when someone you employ uses them and makes you money. Do the work once, get paid back forever.

One risk here is that you look at a process and think, *"There is no use documenting this. It only takes me 5 minutes a day to do it."* You might think it doesn't make sense to invest 20 minutes, creating a *"how-to"* for that process. But if you did, it would save you 5 minutes a day for the rest of your life. Now, does it make sense to start creating *"how-to"* manuals?

The Value in the "How-To" Manual

One of my first clients wanted to retire when I first coached her. She had received an offer for the

Leverage

business, which she had declined. We went to work on the business, and one of the most significant areas of focus for us was building a comprehensive *"how-to"* manual. We did lots of other things, but this manual was the real focus. One year later, she received an offer for 2.3 times more than the previous offer. Did we grow the business by that much in one year? No. What we had done however was create a much more attractive business to investors. They now could buy a business that they would know *"how to"* run. You see, for anyone buying a business, they do not want you around for too long after the sale. They usually demand you be there for at least 12 months to ensure an orderly handover. The risk for them is in that year when the business is still all in your head; you could, God forbid, get hit by a bus. The *"how-to"* manual mitigates that risk to potential purchasers and makes your business much more attractive.

Another client of mine recently sold his business and was dreading the 12-month handover period. Like when an employee is working their notice period, *"Elvis had already left the building."* After the sale went through, my client went into work on day 1 of 365. Yes, he was counting. To his astonishment and delight at lunchtime on day one, the new owners told him that they no longer needed him!!! Our years of documenting everything in his business made this possible. The new owners felt reassured that everything they needed was in the manual. My client was free to begin enjoying his retirement 364.5 days sooner than expected. Not only will creating a *"how-to"* manual save you time now, but it will also be worth a fortune in the future. It will be worth its weight in gold. So, please start on it now. Your future self will thank you for it.

Checklists

Would a pilot take off with 400 passengers on board without going through their checklist? Of course not. By the way, I am not a pilot, yet we try to run a business, which I think is much more complicated than flying a plane, without a checklist. For most business owners, this imaginary *"checklist"* is in their heads. Business owners become exhausted, trying to remember what to do and when to do it. If you ever wake up at 2 am in a cold sweat, thinking if you have forgotten to do something, or scared you will forget to do something, you will understand the need for checklists. Worse still, you wake up worried that others have forgotten to do something or will forget to do something! Every single person in a business, including the owner, needs a checklist. If we move from a people dependant business to a systems dependant business, checklists hold everything together.

An all too common scenario in business is that one of your team calls in sick one day. Typically, after you have cursed them, you proceed in a blind panic thinking how you will ensure all their tasks will happen that day. You rack your brain thinking of all the things they usually do and frantically try to do them. Imagine, instead, stuck to the absent team member's desk is a checklist. You look down and see what they were supposed to do today. Then, you calmly pick up a

Leverage

folder with all their *"how-to"* manuals and simply carry out their tasks. Far too easy some people think, but I promise you it is that easy. And by easy, please do not think simple. Checklists and *"how-to"* manuals take planning and a lot of effort. But remember, do the work once and get paid back forever.

A positive by-product of creating checklists is that we encourage a culture of methodical thinking. People start to automatically say, *"Let us add it to the checklist,"* which is music to my ears. Employees adding to their checklists without being prompted can only be a good thing for how our business runs.

Can you imagine the customer's perception of you when at all stages of their interaction with you, your team refers to the checklist? I promise they will feel more reassured and comfortable doing business with you.

Checklists with everything you do takes all that pressure and stress away. The checklists free you up to concentrate on growing your business.

CHAPTER 13

LEVERAGE SUMMARY

It is important to note that only 80% of your business can be systemised. 20% will always be exceptions that will still need us, humans. Yet, it is impossible to quantify the full value you create when you leverage your business by systemising it. My humble opinion is that it is THE most valuable work you will EVER do. The benefits will last forever, and most importantly, this frees up your time and energy to enjoy your life. Get to work now. Please do not wait!

CHAPTER 14

TEAM

In the Cycle of Business Success, the Team section is my favourite. You see, I am a big believer that most people want to do a good job. There will always be exceptions, but by and large, most people are honest and hardworking and want to do a good job. Our job is to provide them with the environment, tools, and support they need to succeed. It is so sad that most business owners do not want to grow their businesses because they are so sick and tired of trying to manage people, often badly.

Unfortunately, many business owners view people as a number on a spreadsheet. They view them as a cost, an irritation, or a cause of pain. As a big believer in correlations, I believe that you get out of people what you put in. You can go through the motions of managing people. But if your belief system around people is as described above, you will not get out of people what you put in. Your team can either make your life relatively easy or very hard. Which one is it for you? The choice is yours.

You need a system to manage people too. The most important word in management is consistency. Unfortunately, most Managers use their energy and personality to manage people. That management style does not promote consistency, especially if the Manager had a blazing row with their partner before leaving the house that morning. You need a system. I use my 16 Steps to a World-Class Team to create this system. This system helps manage people so that they become an asset to your business, not a liability.

Step 1: Vision

Where are you going? If you do not know the end destination, what is the point in starting the journey? Having a vision for your business is about getting everyone enrolled in where you are going. It should be a short *"punchy"* statement of intent. The vision is where we are going and who we aspire to be. It tells the world about your ambition. It should be something that you will never achieve, but it is something that you will get out of bed every day to try and achieve. It has got to be something that inspires and excites you. For example, here at REACH Business Coaching, our vision is *"To give every business owner a business to be proud of and a life worth living."* Will I ever achieve that? No. But will I be motivated to try? Absolutely!

Internally, the vision sets a standard. An old client of mine had a vision *"to be the best print company in the country."* They had a van that they used to make local deliveries. One day, my client, the MD, noticed the apprentice had washed the outside of the van and was now cleaning the inside. Confused about why this apprentice was wasting time cleaning the inside of the van, my client went to investigate. He inquired, *"Why are you cleaning the inside of the van? Clients only see the outside of the van during deliveries."* The apprentice hesitantly replied, *"Well, if we are going to be the best, the best would clean the inside."* Brilliant! My client, suitably impressed, asked the apprentice to continue cleaning the interior of the van. Design the vision to set a standard amongst your team.

The vision tells everyone who interacts with your business, especially your team, about what standards you aim to achieve. This vision statement should be at the forefront of your recruitment process. More on recruitment later. You should say to any potential candidates, here is our vision. If this does not excite you, do not bother applying.

The vision must come from you, the leader. It is your job to set the course. It is your responsibility to rally the troops to get them excited to follow you. You will not think of the vision overnight. I have found that the more you try and create one, the harder it gets. Relax, put the thought in your subconscious mind, and when it is ready, it will come. And when it does, it will hit you like a sledgehammer. You will feel a rush of electricity go through your body as you know that you are 100% excited by this vision! You would walk through brick walls to achieve it. If the vision statements that come to you do not excite you, forget them and let the next one come to you. This statement has got to get you fired up. It should scare and excite you in equal measures!

Step 2: Mission

Mission shows people in a lot more detail about how you will work towards your vision. What are the things you will do to try and get there? List those activities in the mission. The mission should be a couple of paragraphs long. Do not worry about going into too much detail. I advise you to go as deep as possible to show the world you have thought about this.

The mission statement also comes from you, the leader. Be bold, stretch your comfort zone. Realise that you and the rest of the team will have to grow as individuals, and a collective, to reach your vision.

Step 3: Values

While Values have been mentioned several times already, I thought it best to dedicate a section to showing you how best to go about agreeing on your company values. Before I start on this, let me get one thing straight. The big corporates give the whole Vision, Mission, and Values process a bad name. The big corporates pay expensive consultants to help them craft words and then proceed to tell the entire world how they live by these words. Yet, if you ask one of their employees, most do not even know the Vision, Mission, or Values, never mind how to live and breathe them! My clients create the Vision, Mission, and Values to help them manage the people better, more consistently, not tick a box on a marketing checklist.

The values are the behaviours you will display daily as you work through your mission and strive to arrive at your vision. The values define your DNA. Values are the glue that holds people together. By defining the values, you also create the *"rules of the game"* for daily behaviours. Defining the values creates an unwritten employment contract. For example, if you have a person who arrives at 1 minute to 9 and leaves at exactly 5, then you will know what I mean here. In terms of their contract, they follow it, but they do not play by the spirit of the game. Now, if one of your values were, for example, *"professionalism,"* then I would sit that person down and have a chat with them. I would ask them how showing up a minute before their shift started and leaving bang on time fitted with *"professionalism."* For example, coming in at 1 minute before your work shift started would mean there was no way you could be ready to take a phone call at 9 am. You would not have had time to read and digest any emails or briefings. Having the values allows you to have chats with people about those things that are not necessarily *"black or white."*

Creating values should be a collaborative process. The team must have substantial input when creating values. If you are to hold them accountable to these values, they should play an important part in creating them. They would be much more bought into them if they did.

I advise giving the team the list of values in Appendix 18 at www.theeeplan.com, a list of all values known to humankind. Both you and the team should take these away for a week to mull them over. The intention should be to highlight the 20 most important to you. We want to discover the values the team feels the most passionate to live by in the workplace. Once people have chosen their own top 20 values, you should call a team meeting. The group, through the process of discussion, decide on a final 12-14 maximum. The ideal number is 12, but sometimes it is hard to get everyone's preferences into 12, so in my businesses for example, we ended up with 14. With 12, you should aim for four values that are important to you as the owner. Aim for the four most important values to the team and the four most important to your customers and suppliers.

Start the meeting by tallying up the most popular values chosen by your team. You might want to do the tallying up beforehand to save time. There may be some values determined by everyone, and they will go onto the final list right away. With these and even the values that are not as clear cut, you must have some passionate conversations. You want everyone to understand how important these values will be going forwards; the more vigorous the discussions, the better. Talk about why someone feels particularly strongly about a value. Go deep. It might be something from their personal life, something emotional. This kind of conversation will drive your discussions to a much deeper and meaningful level. What is it about that value that is important to an individual? Is it something that they have seen displayed (or not) in another business? How do you display it / not display it now? What difference would it make if you had that value in the business?

Once you have agreed on the final list of your values, you may want to write a sentence underneath each one to give it more meaning. Some people like to write a sentence underneath. Some do not because they want the value to be wide-ranging and to be able to use it in a variety of different scenarios. They feel that putting a description under it might limit its use. Either way, once you have an agreement, you need to start using the values to hold each other accountable. Try to live and breathe them daily.

For the vision, mission, and values, you must make them visible. If they are not visible, then you have just done what the large corporates do. You simply ticked a box. Remember, these are tools to help you manage people more consistently. Tools left in a toolbox go rusty. My advice is to make them visible in the workplace first. I do not advise making them public just yet. If you do and fall short on something, you can be sure that your customers will point out your failures. Make sure you can *"walk the walk"* before you *"talk the talk."* Have the vision, mission, and values displayed all around you. Do not just stick them on the walls with some Blu Tack. It subconsciously tells the team that you do not take them that seriously. Spend a few pounds getting them made professionally but have them everywhere, so you use them all the time. Once you have confidence that you live and breathe them, then make them public. Get them on the website, get them on the uniforms, put them on your letterheads, business cards, and email signatures. Tell the whole world about them and be proud to shout about them. Show people how passionate you are about these.

Can you imagine putting your values on sales quotes? Can you imagine saying to a prospect, *"Here are our values? If you do not like them, please ignore this quote?"* Do you think that would be a sign that you were serious about your values? If you can do it there, then you do mean it!

By having them visible, you bring in to play the not to be underestimated power of peer to peer accountability. Can you imagine hearing one person hold one of their colleagues accountable if they had deviated from one of the values? If you hear that, you know the values are adding value to the business. And believe me, the customers will see this too.

From now on, whenever you have a tough decision to make, you must use your values as a guide. You will not make decisions that please 100% of the people, 100% of the time. When your head hits the pillow at night, however, you need to know you made all your decisions by your values. That way, you know you have remained consistent, and your integrity is intact.

I have only ever had to fire three clients. Each time has been horrible, but the right thing to do. The first two times, I did not use my values in the decision-making process. So, the following days after sacking the client were not very pleasant. I was questioning myself and beating myself up for possibly hurting the client's feelings. Generally, I did not feel good about myself. The last time I did it, however, I followed up with the client with an email. The email was three paragraphs long. Each paragraph started with one of

Team

our values. I explained how their actions went against our values, so we could not continue working together. Once I sent that email, I felt a real sense of calm. That feeling was unlike the previous two instances where the emotions were negative. I know that the reason for this was that my decision was totally in alignment with our values. I knew that I remained consistent and true to them. The values give you a framework to navigate decisions, especially the tough ones. That is why the values are so important in the *"ABCD"* client grading exercise.

Your gut will tell you if your decisions align with your values. I mentioned this earlier. You will know if you have or have not lived by them automatically. I do not have to say any more about this. You also know when you hire someone, and something did not feel quite right during the recruitment process. Because you did not listen to your gut, more than likely, you had to let them go within the first few months because it just did not work out. Please listen to your gut. It is the best mechanism to ensure that we stay in alignment with our values.

Step 4: Employee Handbook

The employee handbook is a document that has all the necessary legal paperwork in one place. My advice would always be to seek a specialist HR advisor's advice, which will ensure you still have the most up-to-date version of the document. Like Terms and Conditions, it is no use realising that the handbook is not up to date or legally robust enough when you are in an Employment Tribunal. It is too late then!

I would always recommend putting your Vision, Mission, and Values in the handbook. Also, include the individual's Roles and Responsibilities and KPIs (more on that later). Add all the necessary legal documents such as their Employment Contract, Grievance Policy, Maternity/Paternity Policy etc. You want everything in one place. Put your branding on it, and there you have it, a fully loaded Employee Handbook!

Step 5: Organisational Chart

Regardless of the size of your team, you need an Organisational Chart. Everyone needs to know where they fit in the existing setup and who their immediate Line Manager is if they have an issue. The current trend is to have *"flat"* structures, but I am not a fan. Call me old fashioned, but there should be a hierarchy. Can you imagine our armed forces without a chain of command? Everyone needs to know where they fit in the organisation. Also, from a strict HR perspective, if we fire someone, it needs to be done by their Line Manager.

A hierarchical structure also shows people where they can progress in the company if they wish to do so. Most studies have shown that the biggest reason people stay in a job has nothing to do with salary. Their relationship with their Line Manager and opportunities to progress are the most significant reasons for people staying in a role. If you do not have a natural progression path, then you will lose your good people.

Team

When Coaching my clients to create Organisational Charts, I ask them to make 3.

1. The structure as it is today.
2. The structure as you want it in 3 years.
3. The structure as you want it in 5 years.

By creating Organisational Charts for 3 and 5 years, you are setting your RAS, showing your people where they can progress to in the company, and the structure of the company going forwards. Try and colour the boxes that are new roles in different colours to show people the gaps that you hope to fill.

When creating any of these Organisational Charts, I always advise adding some numbers to them. Firstly, what would that structure cost you in payroll terms? Then, what sales could you achieve with that structure? Finally, what is payroll as a percentage of sales? You see, while your business continues to grow and make more sales, it might not become more efficient the bigger you get. What could happen is that the bigger you get, the less efficient you become? Some of my clients see this and realise that there is no use growing past a certain profitability point. Or as growth occurs, it will sharpen the mind in the need for systems and processes to improve efficiencies that drive profitability. I am not saying the amount of profit you make comes down. I am saying that you might be spending disproportionately more on wages the bigger you get. Please do not worry. These numbers will be for your eyes only. The Organisational Chart that you share with the team won't have these numbers on there.

The other bit of advice I will give you is not to let the current team influence what your Organisational Charts should look like in 3 or 5 years. I recommend you do not put people's names in the boxes, just the job titles. That way, if you do have someone in the team who you are not sure if they will be with you in the future, you will not let that get in the way of creating the ideal structure.

The aim of everything you, the business owner does, is to free yourself from the business. So, please do make sure that on one of these Organisational Charts, you have replaced yourself. Freeing yourself might take more than five years, but if you do not have it somewhere on one of the future Organisational Charts, it will never happen.

Turn your Organisational Charts into professional electronic versions with Fiverr.com. Or look in Microsoft Word, Excel, or PowerPoint. Click on *"Insert"* and then *"Shapes"* to create your own.

Please make sure these charts are visible to everyone. The people that are inspired by your vision will naturally approach you and ask questions. Their questions will identify them as people who want to progress and people you can develop for the future. With the right people on the *"bus,"* you can achieve anything.

Step 6: Roles and Responsibilities

"It is not in my job spec." Have you ever heard that

Team

from one of your team when you ask them to do something? Well, now you have the chance to fix this once and for all. It is also essential to give your team clarity on what you expect from them. Do not just assume that they understand through telepathy what it is you want them to do. When completing this exercise with clients, I find most times that their teams are so thankful to know what is expected of them finally! Let us get everything written down so that there are no *"grey"* areas. The grey areas are where the issues typically begin.

Now that you have Organisational Charts, you know the Roles and Responsibilities documents you need to write. And before you ask, yes, you should write out the ones for future roles as well.

Start with you. What does, or should, the owner do? I have a little hint for you. Think of the £500 per hour jobs first. List them down to start with, and then you can add as much detail as you want later. Get excited about delegating some of the things you know you should not do, and do not like doing, to other people. Indulge yourself a little and give yourself some £8 per hour jobs that you like to do because you can enjoy yourself a little!

Once you have yours drafted, work down the Organisational Chart. Create first drafts of everyone else's Roles and Responsibilities. If you get stuck, then Google those roles. You will find recruitment sites hiring for those jobs, and you can get ideas from there. It is sometimes useful to Google *"Managing*

Director" job descriptions too. You might find it quite enlightening!

Now share the documents with the relevant individuals for them to take away and review. Give them a week to *"chew it over."* Then, meet to discuss their thoughts with them. This meeting is private, just them and you. Their feedback might mean you change some job descriptions a little. Either way, the goal is for them to sign off on these Roles and Responsibilities.

The team members with the right mindset will give constructive feedback and add other things into the mix. The team members that are not engaged will simply nod and accept whatever you put in front of them. Either way, everyone should have the opportunity to give input into the creation of this document.

Some of my clients also ask their teams to create their Roles and Responsibilities simultaneously, and then they can sit down and compare notes between their document and yours.

Going back to the first words in this section, you need to ensure you do not create a culture of *"it is not in my job spec."* Do that by including one line in the Roles and Responsibilities documents that says, *"To carry out any reasonable request from your Line Manager to meet business needs."* Let us say, for example, you are in retail, and one morning there are leaves or snow outside the shop, creating the potential for a customer to slip. You should be able to ask one of your team to go and clean the debris without risking the *"it's not in my job spec"* reply. Think of it as a *"catch-all."* PS – if you

Team

make a reasonable request and one of your team does not carry it out, then this is classed as Insubordination. In most instances, the UK classifies Insubordination as Gross Misconduct. Gross Misconduct could result in disciplinary action against the individual. As managers, you need to know that.

Once you and the team have agreed on the Roles and Responsibilities, all parties understand expectations. Remember, make it as clear as possible because ambiguity will hurt further down the line.

Step 7: Key Performance Indicators

KPI's (Key Performance Indicators) drive behaviour. If you are not getting the right kinds of behaviours you are looking for, then revisit the KPI. When a farmer is trying to herd the sheep into a pen, they normally enlist the help of a sheepdog. They get the sheepdog to follow their instructions through a dog whistle, ensuring that the sheep reach their pen safely. For me (please don't think I'm referring to our team as dogs!), the KPI's are the dog whistle.

Without a doubt, this is the most complicated and frustrating part of the Team section in the Cycle of Business Success. Everyone in the business needs KPI's, including you. They measure performance. They give everyone absolute clarity on what is expected. The KPI's cannot have any areas of doubt. They must be achieved or not achieved. Yes or no. Binary, 0 or 1, black or white. I will repeat it; they cannot have any areas of doubt. The reason will become apparent soon.

Over the years, I have been guilty of over-complicating this area. At one stage, I had some client's team members on over 10 KPI's per month. 10 KPI's is impractical, leads to a lack of focus in any one area, and to be honest; it is not fair on anyone. Assigning 10 KPI's to an individual creates a definite Lose-Lose. What I teach is that everyone should have a maximum of 3 KPI's. Some may have 2, some may only have 1, but I believe the most should be 3.

They should come under these three categories:

1. **Money** – I believe everyone in the business should have a KPI related to money. Ideally, profit, but something that everyone should focus on in the business should be money. It could be a sales target. It could be the gross profit percentage. Be careful of the team members who say that they cannot influence profit because, for example, they work in Administration. If they do not send the invoices out correctly and on time, this will affect profit. Everyone influences profit. On the subject of profit, if you currently reward your sales team on sales, please change this to gross margin instead. A lazy salesperson can make lots of money discounting to hit their sales targets while the business makes no money.

2. **Customer** – I believe everyone in the business should have a KPI related to the customer. It could be delivering the product on time. It could be a customer satisfaction score. Assigning a KPI

related to a customer satisfaction score would, of course, mean having to create a Customer Satisfaction Questionnaire. Let us say there were ten questions on this questionnaire where the customer gives a rating between 1-10. The KPI could be that the total scores at the end of the month need to be 80 or above.

3. **Internal** – I believe that everyone in the business should have a KPI related to an internal system or process that you need them to follow. What needs to happen to ensure everything runs smoothly? Could it be submitting their timesheets accurately and on time? Could it be following a checklist 100% of the time? Having a KPI in this area gives even more focus to your aim of becoming a system driven business, not a people-driven one.

Again, when we have defined the KPI's, we should consult with the team members. We need to allow them to add, subtract, and amend. Once we have been through the consultation period, add the KPI's to the Roles and Responsibilities. Give each team member their document. Again, let them take it away for a few days to review it and set a deadline for returning it to you. Once they have agreed, get them to sign two copies: one for them and one for you. Never underestimate the power of a pen and a signature on a piece of paper when it comes to accountability. As soon as an individual puts their signature on a document, they own it. If they refuse to sign the Roles and Responsibilities and KPI's document, then please discuss this with your HR advisor about the next steps to take. I would not want to give legal advice. My view is crystal clear; no one individual is more significant than the team. If one individual thinks they are the exception, it undermines your efforts to build a world-class team. The team is always more important than one individual.

When a new person joins the team, during the Induction Process, give them this document to sign too. With your existing team, it might be harder to get everyone enrolled into a new process, however, there is no excuse for not getting buy in from new people, from day one.

Another area to just touch on is the fear and worry my clients have of getting the KPI's wrong. This fear of failure and desire for perfection leads to procrastination. Procrastination leads to inaction. At the start of this section, I said KPI's drive behaviour. Sometimes, with the best will in the world, we end up getting the wrong behaviours. In all my experience coaching thousands of clients, no one has ever got the KPI's right the first time. You mitigate this risk by explaining to the team with absolute humility that you are new to setting KPI's. Explain further that you do not expect to get it right the first time. So, you reserve the right to change these KPI's as many times as you want in the first six months. That way, you do have a bit of *"wiggle"* room if you need to change things. Going forwards, I would not change KPIs any more than quarterly, and even then, only if absolutely necessary. You must allow your team to achieve what you ask of them, and you are not giving them much of a chance if you keep moving the *"goalposts."*

What I find virtually every single time we do this is that the team members are so grateful to know what it is you want them to do finally. They appreciate knowing how you will measure performance. They want to feel secure in the knowledge that they are doing a good job.

Step 8: 1-2-1's

In the Team section of the Cycle of Business Success, I recognise 1-2-1's as the most critical area. It is where everything we have done before comes together. It helps you to finally manage your people properly. It is the one time every month where you or the team member's Line Manager will sit down with them in private so that all parties can see how they are doing. If you currently do the dreaded Annual Appraisal, you will be pleased to know that you can now stop doing them! Just for the record, the Annual Appraisal is such a waste of time and paper. Most people forget what they had for breakfast that day. But managers think that they will remember everything they did in the last 12 months, and will be able to turn that into a meaningful discussion! What you should be doing is having a monthly 1-2-1 with everyone so that you can course-correct as you go.

The 1-2-1's are done monthly or weekly if you are managing salespeople. A month is a long time for a salesperson to be having a bad time and you not knowing it! 1-2-1's should take no more than an hour.

You might be wondering about the merits of finding 12 hours a year for each of your direct reports. The Annual Appraisal consumed only 2 to 3 hours of your time, after all. As mentioned in the previous paragraph, you must weigh up the benefit of a regular update versus the annual update that serves no purpose. Remember, for each hour you spend with one of your team; you will save yourself at least 10 hours that month not having to give ongoing feedback/management.

During that one hour:

- Give feedback, especially on the KPIs.
- Listen to concerns, document them.
- Coach them up, agree training needs.

You will not have to engage in a firefight and *"manage in the moment"* management style if the 1-2-1s happen every month. Does it not make sense to invest quality time in your team to result in a win-win for all parties? PS – your answer to this question will tell you a lot about your relationship with people and how much you value them. If you do not see the value in giving time to your people, then hire someone who will do it for you. Then all you must do is that new person's 1-2-1. If that is the case, then the person doing the 1-2-1's in your stead should take 2 hours a month reporting to you. The first hour should be them giving you updates on all the 1-2-1's they have done for the team that month to keep you in the loop. The second hour is about them and their performance.

Team

You will need to create a form to use in the 1-2-1. This form will ensure consistency for the individual every month. Also, you will maintain consistency for other areas of the business if you have different managers doing 1-2-1's. You can find an example of a 1-2-1 form in Appendix 19 at www.theeeplan.com, but you might want to create your own. Do not look to make the perfect form before starting your 1-2-1's. Like most things, you will undoubtedly have to amend the form based on your learnings as you do more and more 1-2-1's. Just get started and show your team how much you value them and how much of your time you are prepared to invest in them. For the most part, this will pay you back.

I mentioned the importance of consistency in the 1-2-1's earlier, especially if more than one person is doing them in the business. If you have a management structure below you, in the long term, the Managers will do their team's 1-2-1's. Then you will only do the Manager(s). In the first instance however, I suggest you, as the leader, do all the 1-2-1's. I know this will take your time, but I promise it will be worth it. After you have done a couple of months 1-2-1's, invite the individual's Line Manager into the next 1-2-1 to observe you conducting the 1-2-1. The following month ask the Line Manager to conduct the 1-2-1 while you observe. If you are happy, then the month after you leave them to it. Just to ensure that you delegate (and not abdicate), I suggest periodically sitting in on random 1-2-1's to ensure their consistency. Once you do the 1-2-1's with consistency, please record some of them for the *"how-to"* manuals.

The 1-2-1 should focus on the team member's wellbeing and concerns. Also, consider both inside and outside of work conversations. Focus the majority of the 1-2-1 however, on the KPI's. You, as their Manager, should coach them on how to achieve the KPI's they have not hit in the previous month. Please do not forget to recognise them for achieving the ones that they did hit. You might want them to coach someone else in the team that is struggling in this area for example. Regardless, spend most of the time on the KPI's because if everyone achieves 100% of their KPI's, they will fly, and so will your business. What better use of your time could there be than to get your team performing?

Please prepare beforehand, so you have their KPI's for the previous month and year to date. One tactic I have used is to have a password-protected document on my laptop for every one of my direct reports for that month. During the month, whenever I see something good or bad, I note it on this document. I take this document in with me to the 1-2-1, so I will not get frustrated because I forgot to mention something that I was desperate to discuss in the 1-2-1. Again, mention the good stuff, too; catch them doing something good. The time you have for the 1-2-1 is the most valuable time you will have with that individual, so it makes sense to prepare for it, so you get the most out of that time.

Start to get used to channelling all your feedback through the 1-2-1. As I said, document it and save it for the 1-2-1. Yet, if there is a *"code red,"* such as you

Team

heard the team member swearing at a customer on the phone, that cannot wait. You need to address all *"code red"* situations immediately. Everything else should wait for the 1-2-1.

Some other house rules:

- Schedule the 1-2-1's in the first week of every month so that the previous month is still relatively fresh in everyone's memory.
- Position the 1-2-1 as being just as much for them as it is for you. This is their time with their Line Manager.
- Put them in the diary as a recurring appointment for the following 12 months.
- Do not ever cancel one unless there is a fire in the building. By fire, I mean an actual fire with flames! Imagine what message it sends to your team if you cancel their 1-2-1? Get it in your Default Diary and stick to it.
- The individual's Line Manager should conduct the 1-2-1.
- I always ask my direct reports to email me at least one thing that they want to discuss in their 1-2-1 at least 24 hours before it is due to happen. For example, if they want to discuss their pay, at least I can check their records to see when they got their last pay rise in advance of the 1-2-1.
- Document EVERYTHING. You MUST have an audit trail of every conversation, especially if

they are not hitting their KPI's. What training did they ask you to provide? What coaching did you give them? What have they expressed as their hopes and ambitions for the future, and how can you help them become the best versions of themselves? Document everything!

- Type up your notes if your handwriting is terrible.
- Again, get them to sign two copies, one for them and one for you.
- If there were actions, start the next 1-2-1 with them. If any of those actions are for you, then it is an absolute priority that you have done them. You have zero credibility trying to hold them accountable for not doing something when you have not done what you were supposed to do. Put the time in your Default Diary for completing 1-2-1 actions.

Years ago, one of my clients had ongoing issues with one of their team members. When he began conducting the 1-2-1's, the problems disappeared. Several months later, during a coaching session, the client mentioned that he had more issues with the team member. Surprised, I asked him, *"How did this happen?"* because 1-2-1's should prevent issues occurring with consistent and open dialogue. My client said he had stopped doing the 1-2-1's as soon as things had improved between him and the team member! I explained, never stop the 1-2-1's. In good times and not so good times, they must continue to happen.

I sincerely hope you fully embrace the importance of doing 1-2-1's as a proactive tool to help manage people. The first 1-2-1 blows most people away. They feel valued that their Line Manager would invest their precious time in them. The participation in 1-2-1's leads to a much deeper and rewarding relationship for all parties and the all-important win-win.

Step 9: Performance Management

I coach lots of different clients in lots of various industries with lots of varying challenges. The coaching involves discussions and invariably compromises. One thing that I cannot compromise on, however, is team members that do not perform. These non-performers are known as *"deadwood."* I have seen businesses brought to their knees because management does not deal with non-performers. Instead, the business owner hopes that the problem will go away. They sometimes console themselves by thinking that out of the ten team members, nine are tremendous, and there is only 1 *"bad egg."* Sooner or later, those 9 *"superstars"* will get frustrated by their one colleague who does not pull his weight because those *"superstars"* have to *"pick up the slack."* How long before they get disenfranchised? How long before they think, *"Why should I bother?"* Not long, I promise you. When that happens, you will have ten problems, not 1.

Let us not sugarcoat this. People think if you bury your head in the sand, it might go away. I hate to be the bearer of bad news; it will not go away on its own. Instead, it grows like a tumour, and unless treated, it will kill your business. You can do whatever else you want to grow your business, but this *"thing"* will make you terminally ill.

One of the biggest reasons business owners do not deal with *"deadwood"* is that they do not know how or fear doing it wrong and ending up in court. In my corporate career, I had to dismiss 17 people. I needed to deal with these 17 horrible situations. I affected 17 livelihoods; 17 gut-wrenching experiences. 17 times I could have been in an Employment Tribunal but was not. The reason for this is because I followed the system.

Yes, I was in large companies with HR departments to support me, but you have that support all around you now, so there is no excuse not to act.

You received information on the system in the preceding pages. It starts with clearly defined Roles and Responsibilities and KPI's. Every month the performance is reviewed in the 1-2-1. If the individual does not achieve the KPI's, then a conversation is documented in the 1-2-1 to decide what all parties will do to correct this. The Line Manager gives the necessary support in the form of coaching and training. If, after all that, the KPI's are still not being hit, then, unfortunately, you must move to the next stage of the system, which is a Disciplinary Hearing. The outcome of this hearing may be to place the individual on a Performance Improvement Plan. The Performance Improvement Plan is a detailed document, which will highlight what they must do to hit the KPI's. If, after all this, the KPI's are still not met, then with regret and a heavy heart, because you are dealing with someone's livelihood, you must dismiss them. Please note the Disciplinary Hearing part of the process must be in line with your Employment Contracts. So, please make sure you get specialist HR advice.

It is never a nice feeling to have to dismiss someone, especially if they have tried their best and are a nice person. When you dismiss someone, it is vital to look in the mirror and know that you did everything possible to help that person succeed. If you have, then although it does not feel nice, you must console yourself that you have done the right thing. You feel sad about the livelihood you have just affected; however, you might have affected everyone else's livelihood in the business, including your own, if you had not acted. Most times, when the person has left, your team will tell you how relieved they are that the person has left. They then tell you about another 100 things the dismissed person did wrong that you did not even know about! Also, dealing with *"deadwood"* sends a message to the rest of the team that you are serious about performance. If people in your team do not hit the mark, you are not a daycare centre for adults, but a business. It is your duty and responsibility to act.

The example I just described hinted at going through this process monthly in the 1-2-1s. For some reading this book, that might seem too long to wait when dealing with *"deadwood,"* and for the most part, it is. You need to balance the business's needs with the need to give the individual enough time to hit their KPI's.

That said, and in consultation with your HR advisor, you can hurry matters and move the milestones to fortnightly or even weekly.

I have seen many examples where a person should not be in a position and is left sometimes for decades to continue. These persons do not even perform the basics of their role and get away with it every day. Owners and managers cite a lack of time to deal with them and a need for their knowledge in the business, as the reasons not to dismiss under-performing team members. Under-performing team members with essential business information stored in their heads give you even more reason to get systems and processes in place. My terrified clients often ask, *"What happens if they leave?"* I respond with, *"What happens if they stay?"*

One thing I have seen business owners do is to abdicate their responsibilities and use the *"redundancy"* route to remove someone who is not performing. Now let me be clear; this is much quicker and easier than the long drawn out, and emotionally draining performance management process. My observation on this strategy is that while it might be easier for you in the short term, it is flawed. For example, what message does this send to the rest of the team? Do not perform for years, and instead of being held to account, you will get a big payoff to leave? Not a particularly good message, I hope you agree! When someone has done so much harm to the business, why should they get even more money? Also, as a manager, you are not learning the full performance management process unless you go all the way through it. Choosing the redundancy route is merely burying your head in the sand, which is *"denial"* and below the line.

When dismissing people, you must give them feedback on their development areas. You do not want them to make the same mistakes in their next role.

Thoroughly and professionally managing people sends all the right messages to the team. Send the message that you have a standard that you expect all your people to hit, and if they do not, you will hold them to account.

I want to complete the section on performance management by repeating what I said at the start. No business I have ever worked with has ever moved forwards, let alone achieved its objectives by holding on to *"deadwood."* It is scary, stressful, time-consuming, and energy-draining, but you must act. You have no choice.

I have now given you the system. It is up to you to get *"above the line,"* feel the *"perturbation,"* and act. After all, as a client of mine once said, *"It is better to have a hole in your business than an arsehole."* Please forgive the salty language.

Step 10: Reward and Recognition

Performance management is about when people do not hit their KPI's. Reward and recognition is about what you do when they do. You can say performance management was the *"stick,"* and reward and recognition is the *"carrot."*

All the research has shown that people crave recognition more than reward. Being acknowledged as having excelled amongst your peer group is more important than any kind of monetary reward. So, please give plenty of thought to the recognition aspect of any scheme you may introduce. *"Team Member of the Month"* can carry so much more weight for people than a bonus in their wages.

That said, I want to illustrate how easy it is to create a reward and recognition scheme in your business. As mentioned before, people should have max 3 KPI's. In the example of someone having 3 KPI's, at the end of every month, they will have one of four possible scores; 0%, 33%, 66%, or 100%. Those results assume that the Line Managers score the KPI's as described previously, with no ambiguity. They either hit the KPI, or they did not. In the 1-2-1, you log these scores in a spreadsheet. See Appendix 20 at www.theeeplan.com. This spreadsheet gives the individual their year to date scores too so that when the year ends, their overall score is not a surprise. After all, you updated them every month in their 1-2-1, and the majority of the 1-2-1 was dedicated to you helping them achieve the KPI's.

At the year-end, when it comes to deciding who gets what pay rise, you can take the individual's KPI score and create a matrix like this:

- 80% to 100% = 5% pay rise + cost of living increase.
- 60% to 79% = 3% pay rise + cost of living increase.

Team

- Less than 59% = cost of living increase.

You can use the same principles to determine the bonus scheme if you have one. You can dedicate a percentage of profit every month to a bonus pot. An individual's annual KPI scores will determine what percentage they receive of the bonus pool.

Bonus Scheme:

- 80% to 100% = 5% bonus.
- 60% to 79% = 3% bonus.
- Less than 59% = 0% bonus.

For the bonus, you can decide the frequency of the payouts. It may be annually, quarterly, bi-annually, or even monthly. The choice is yours.

You can have either of these schemes or both. Everything that an individual does daily is reviewed and discussed in their monthly 1-2-1. Now, their daily performance has a bearing on what they receive from you in their wages.

You have many great reasons to adopt a similar scheme but let me give you a scare into doing this too. Are you someone who gives out discretionary bonuses to people? If you are, you will be like most business owners. Imagine giving Bob 5 and John 10. Imagine Bob finds out, which he will. Bob asks, *"Why did I only get 5 while John got 10?"* If you do not have a documented scheme justifying this, then theoretically, Bob can claim discrimination. I know that sounds far-fetched, and some of you may think I am scaremongering, but rest assured, it happens. We mitigate this risk by having a scheme in place.

If you have ever given out a blanket pay rise or bonus, you will know that some people in your team deserve more than others. Again, because you do not have a scheme in place, you must give everyone the same, which frustrates you. This policy could de-motivate your superstars who do not feel valued. Especially if you gave the same reward to *"deadwood."* By having a scheme in place, at least you reward the people based on their performance.

Some business owners think a reward and recognition scheme will be complicated and time-consuming to administer. I hope I have shown you how simple it is to put into place if you have already carried out the previous steps.

Allow me to share one final caveat on any reward and recognition schemes. I come across many different businesses that are paying all their team members great bonuses, and significant annual pay rises. Most times, the person creating the scheme does not think it through to the end, resulting in everyone making money, except the business. You should build in a safety mechanism to protect the business. We stated that everyone in the business might hit 100% of their KPI's. Yet, if the business does not hit its profit target, then no bonuses should be paid. Possibly the only pay rises will be the cost of living increases. This way of approaching pay increases and bonuses may sound harsh, but as the business's custodian and guardian, you must make tough calls to protect it.

You also want to avoid creating silos. What can happen is where one department that has hit all their KPI's takes their *"foot off the gas."* That department relaxes while another department is struggling and will not hit their KPI's. What you want is an environment where the *"coasting"* department immediately goes to the struggling department to give help, because they know that if the struggling team do not hit their KPI's, the possibility exists that no one will get paid bonuses or pay rises.

Step 11: Recruitment

Professional recruitment agencies tell me that *"traditional"* recruitment only gives you a 50/50 chance of finding the right candidate. I will say that again in case you think you misread. By going through the traditional route (CV and interview), you have just as much chance of getting it wrong as you have of getting it right. Wow! This method is littered with risk. Most people read a CV that could have been written by someone who is not even the candidate. And you could interview someone who could have been coached by someone else on how to *"ace"* interviews. They use these two fundamentally flawed and open to abuse processes to make 99% of their decision. Madness! When the successful candidate starts working for you, you realise that they are not anything like the person you took through the recruitment process. No wonder so many people say to me, *"Jas, I just cannot get good people!"* With this kind of approach, it is no surprise!

The other colossal drawback with traditional recruitment is the time it takes. How often have you sat down to begin an interview and realised immediately that the candidate is not a good fit, but out of respect, you go through the entire interview process? This approach to recruiting is incredibly time consuming and frustrating. And still, you only have a 50/50 chance of getting the right person.

I see disillusioned business owners who are so tired of trying to find good people. They are so tired of having only ever found *"average"* or *"below average"* people that all their hopes and ambitions for their business grind to a halt. *"To hell with it, I will just go back to being me on my own. It was easier that way!"* What a crying shame. When you have good people in your business, you see possibilities and excitement about the future. When you have *"deadwood,"* all you see is hard work and a constant battle to get people to do what you ask. Sound familiar?

You will be pleased to know that there is another way. A step by step process that, if followed, will give you a 90% success rate of getting the right person, first time. Primarily, my recruitment process is based on attitude, not aptitude. How many times have you come across someone who has all the certificates and qualifications but cannot even make eye contact? After all, you cannot teach attitude. You either have it, or you don't. Alongside attitude, my process is also based on values. Do they match yours? Will they be a good fit? My process allows candidates to de-select themselves. De-selected candidates decide that what you have asked them to do is too much trouble for them. They de-select themselves because they cannot be bothered to step outside of their comfort zones. The process, as described next, will save you so much valuable time. People de-selecting themselves means you do not have to waste time on them. Every single step you will learn about is in the process for a reason. Leave one step out because you think it is not important, and your chances of getting the right person the first time revert to a 50/50 chance.

Stage 1 – The Job Advert

The job advert is intended to be vague. It focuses on behavioural attributes as opposed to technical requirements. The job ad asks interested parties to call an 0845 number. For those non-UK readers, this is a number that is classed as non-geographic and is included in most people's mobile phone call plans. It allows flexible routing of calls and does not tie you to any geographic location. This number is rented by you on a monthly basis, from telecom companies.

Post the job ad on the standard job websites, unless the role you are recruiting for is a real niche role with a specific recruitment website(s). Most websites will not let you post a job without uploading an application form. As my process does not require an application form, the workaround for this is to create a Word document with one line in it, repeating what was in the job ad, *"Please call 0845 XXXXXX to apply."*

Stage 2 – Voice Recording

When the candidates call the number, they hear a voice message from you. It thanks them for the call and reminds them again about the role, hours, and location. You then say, *"If you want to be considered for the next stage of the recruitment process, please leave me a 30-60 second message saying what you would bring to the role. Please remember to leave your contact details."*

What do most people who hear that message do? Yes, they hang up!! They de-select themselves. Some go away, compose themselves, prepare what they will say, and call the number again. They leave a well thought out message. That shows resourcefulness, and I have no issue with that; I think it's great!

The other advantage of candidates calling the 0845 number is that you will not have your phone lines jammed by people asking questions about the job! Every time a message is left, you receive it in your email. Simply filter the emails with the voice messages into a separate folder, which means they will not clog up your inbox.

Stage 3 – Review the Messages

Once the deadline you set for applicants to leave messages has passed, grab yourself a cuppa, and sit down. Go to the folder where you stored the emails with the voice messages. Usually, the email subject has the duration of the message in it. How many messages you have received will determine what you do next. If you have more than 20, for example, then you need to be quite harsh. You may recall the answerphone message stated that you wanted the message to be between 30 to 60 seconds. I usually discount any messages that are less than 25 seconds and more than 65 seconds. If you are going to be a systems driven business, you need people to follow systems. If people cannot follow basic instructions now, what will they be like when they are in the business? I know it sounds harsh, but every step in the process is there for a reason. If you only have a handful of voicemails however, you will undoubtedly have to be more lenient in this part of the process and review all of the messages instead.

Once you have decided how many messages you will listen to, start listening. Can you feel the energy and a buzz in their voices? Yes, it matters what they say, but at this stage, be more interested in how they say it.

Once you have picked your favourites, call them, congratulating them for proceeding to the next stage. Inform them the next step requires a 15-minute (maximum) telephone screening interview. Schedule the screening interview for the following day at one of several set times. Once they have chosen a time, thank them and finish the call.

Stage 4 – Telephone Screening Interview

On this call, ask them previously set questions you have prepared. Ask anything specifically related to the job now. Ask some qualifying questions about their current job, what their notice period is, and if they drive.

Then, ask them to email you their CV. When you receive it, tell them you will email them your list of Company Values. Instruct them to rate themselves on a scale of 1 to 10 for each value. Furthermore, instruct them to write one sentence for each value in their own handwriting, justifying each score. For example, 8 out of 10 for the value *"Professionalism." "Once, when working in a shop, a customer walked in at 4.59pm (we closed at 5pm), and I waited and served them for 40 minutes."* You ask them to bring this document with them to the next stage of the recruitment process.

The next stage will be held at your offices on Sunday at 9am. Yes, Sunday at 9am! You tell them that you will be doing a short presentation on the company and the role. Then you will be asking each candidate to come up to the front of the room, in front of everyone, including the other candidates. You inform them that each candidate will give a 2-minute talk on why they should get the job. You tell them that there will be some other exercises, both group, and individual. Thank them and finish the call.

Stage 5 – The Recruitment Morning

It is best to have this at your offices, but if you cannot, or do not have offices, then hire a hotel boardroom for the morning.

Team

While everyone in Step 4 told you they would be there, less than 25% will show up , and to be honest, you only want about 25% of the candidates showing up so you can really study and assess them! You are testing to see if people have the desire to join your team. If they cannot be bothered to get out of bed on Sunday morning and stretch their comfort zones, they cannot help you move your business forward. Most people's number one phobia is public speaking, and number two is death! So, the people who have shown up on Sunday morning have told you that they are hungry. For me, desire, not ability, determines success in life. With these kinds of people in our team, we can achieve anything.

Start the session by doing a quick PowerPoint presentation. You tell them about where you have come from, where you are, and where you want to go. You tell them about the role and the type of person you want to fill the position. Next, show a slide that shows all the things that have frustrated you when hiring people in the past. These are my points of frustration I make during the presentation:

- 9am means 8.45am, and 5pm means whenever the work is done.
- We are a small business, and we clean the office, and we empty the bins.
- We do not eat while talking on the phone.

You may have others, add them to this slide, because the next slide is in the biggest font possible. It asks, *"Does anyone want to leave?"* No one does leave, but what you have done is create a *"contract"* with the people. If they are successful and join your team and ever deviate from the standards, you show them this slide again. You remind them that the PowerPoint slide outlined the *"Rules of the Game."* You remind them that they accepted them by not leaving the room that Sunday morning when you gave them the opportunity to do so. Once you have spoiled your child, it is tough, if not impossible, to correct the behaviour. The same is true with adults. So, make it clear right at the start exactly what you expect of them.

Once you complete the presentation, ask which candidate wants to come to the front of the room and talk first. I have a scoring matrix for every stage of the process, even the steps before Sunday morning. I always give an extra mark to the person who stood up first because that takes real strength. Once everyone has spoken, ask all candidates to complete a Behavioural Profiling Questionnaire. We use DISC. Print out the questionnaires in advance and have plenty of pencils available.

Then undertake some tasks related to the role itself. For example, if you are hiring an Office Administrator, ask them to complete some basic Word and Excel tasks. Yes, you will need some laptops in the room.

Then engage in some group discussions to assess people's communication and interpersonal skills. Sit the candidates at a table to discuss business topics. As topics of discussion, I use *"the importance of processes in a business,"* and *"the importance of customers."* You will no doubt think of lots of different questions to test their interpersonal skills, and that is fine. While what they say is important, what is most important is how they say it and how they engage with others. Did you have someone who said nothing? Did you have someone who talked over everyone? Did you have someone who expressed their views and then asked others for their opinions and facilitated a discussion?

Once this discussion is over, you ask if they have any questions and then let them go. The morning session should typically last no more than 2 hours.

Then do a *"wash up"* and total up the scores in the scoring matrix for all candidates. Then process the Behavioural Profile Questionnaires online. Only input the questionnaires for candidates that have high scores because the reports will cost you money. Once the reports come back, it usually reinforces your decision.

After calling the successful candidate to give the good news, call or email the unsuccessful ones and give them the bad news. Tell them where they were outscored and where they need to improve. That is your duty and responsibility.

Once documented the first time, this entire process will never take you more than half a day in its entirety every time you want to recruit someone in the future. Remember, do the work once, get paid back forever. If you follow every step, you will get the right person 90% of the time, the first time. If you miss even one step in the recruitment process, the odds go back to 50/50.

When first explaining this process to someone, they think I am from another planet. The approach is so counter-intuitive, it throws people into a daze. Yet, if you have ever hired someone and it has not worked out, then what have you got to lose? How else can you put people in a state of *"perturbation"* to test them? You definitely cannot test people properly when you sit across from them in an interview!

Here are some more points to consider about the process:

- You will notice that other than the call in Step 4, there was not an interview. If the role is more technical, then you can, of course, add another step to the process. You can invite the successful candidate(s) back for a formal technical assessment/interview after the recruitment morning.

- During the recruitment morning, if you or someone else get a chance, look inside each candidate's car. They say that you can tell a lot about a person by looking at their bathroom and car!

- If you can, get a couple of your clients to attend the recruitment morning to observe. Your clients will give you a different perspective and one that you cannot afford to ignore.

- If possible, take your preferred candidate out for lunch before offering them the job. How people treat the bar and the waiting staff tells you EVERYTHING about their values.

Team

- Before making any decision, make sure your team has had a part to play in the process. Whether your team attends the recruitment morning, or for example, you ask the candidate to come in and spend a morning with them. Get feedback from your team.

- If you feel confident enough, at the start of the process, instead of a voicemail, ask candidates to send a 2-minute video of themselves instead. I once recruited a Marketing Manager and did precisely this. I felt that if they cannot market themselves by producing a video, then how will they be able to market my business?

- Never take the best of a bad bunch. Selecting the best candidate from a poor group is an easy trap to fall into, especially when you are busy and need to get someone in urgently. We have all been guilty of this, but let me ask you a question, when has this ever been successful? If the candidate leading on the scoring matrix has not blown you away, then start again. I know this is so hard, but remember the old saying, "Hire slow, fire fast."

- The people my clients have hired tell us that the quirky hiring process compelled them to apply for the position. So, if you want forward-thinking people, embrace the forward-thinking and slightly crazy recruitment process.

I have been teaching this process for years. To provide more context, I would like to share some experiences relative to this recruitment process. I hope these experiences will reinforce why my hiring process is better than *"traditional"* recruitment.

A client of mine was a mechanic. He expressed concern that we could not ask a mechanic to do a presentation. My view is that everyone should be able to stand at the front of the room and talk. In this instance, I decided to compromise. While we were not going to ask candidates to do a presentation, we would ask them to come in at 9am on a Sunday to show us how they did an oil change. Yes, we would observe how they did the oil change, but more importantly, were they sufficiently hungry for this job to leave their beds at 9am on a Sunday? That is the key point here. Do not overthink the individual tasks I have listed. Think more about how you will test to see if they want this job.

After explaining this process to a new client, he said, *"If we had had this process in our business, hardly any of the existing team would currently be here."* He realised what he had said before he had even finished the sentence. I simply smiled and nodded.

Years ago, during recruitment for a Marketing Manager in our own business, after the morning, we were unable to split two candidates. As mentioned previously, it is okay to add an extra step(s). We asked both candidates to prepare a PowerPoint presentation on what they would do in their first 12 months as Marketing Manager. Thirty minutes before the scheduled second session, one candidate called to ask for the session to be postponed to a later date. I asked, *"Why?"* She replied, *"I did not have enough time to prepare the presentation."* I told her that we had a duty to see the other candidate. If the other candidate were not successful, we would let her know. In hindsight, I fell short on my values. I was not honest with her. She had already de-selected herself by her actions, and I should have said that. So, the only candidate left in the running arrived to do the presentation. Unfortunately, on all the slides, he had spelled the name of our business wrong!!! You may be surprised to hear that this was not why he did not get the job. The reason he was not successful was that when I pointed out his error, he was unable to regain his composure. Failure to regain his composure led me to believe that he would struggle under pressure (perturbation). Where could I have created that environment in *"traditional"* recruitment?

To emphasise why attitude and desire are so important, I will share with you a great example from a book called *"Delivering Happiness"* by Tony Hsieh. In his company called Zappos, people would have a 6-week induction and training programme when joining the company. At the end of week 1, Zappos offered all the people in the training room $2,000 to leave. Every week, Zappos added another $2,000 to the *"reward"* to entice trainees to leave. Meaning at the end of the six weeks, people have an offer of $12,000 to go. Some leave, but of the ones that stay, Zappos knows they are here for the right reasons, and empires can be built with these kinds of people in the team.

In summary, so many business owners that I know are so sick and tired of not finding good people that they give up. They make do with substandard people and have accepted their destiny is to spend all their time and energy trying to bring them up to standard. As a believer in correlations, if you put more time into recruitment, you will get better results. The process I have outlined takes a fraction of the time of the traditional recruitment process. Remember, your people will either make your life relatively easy or very hard!

Step 12: Induction

I see so much time and even more energy put into the recruitment process with zero thought given to what happens when that person starts. Can you imagine being the person who went through that recruitment process? It is fair to think that they would think that this is a serious company when it comes to performance. The successful candidate would think, *"I'd better bring my 'A game' to the party every day."* They then show up for their first day, and you have not even remembered they were starting today! Can you imagine what they think now?!

I once started a job and was told to figure things out for the first week! First impressions last, and this is one instance where you must get things right.

My preference, as per Michael Gerber in the

"E-Myth" is that they sit down with the owner for the first morning. Your job as the owner is to share with the new team member the vision, mission, and values. They already should know about the vision, mission and values because that would have come up in the recruitment process, but you should go deeper. Give them your take on the world. Tell them about your life story. Tell them the experiences that have shaped you. Explain how those experiences shape your view on the world today and how they manifest themselves in the business.

Once they complete all the orientation requirements, present them with a work timetable (Default Diary) for at least the first week. Give them a structure of where they will be and what they will be doing. Ideally, they should at least spend time with every person and every department in the business. Have them report their observations to their Line Manager daily.

Another thing I like my clients to do when a new person starts is to stress test their systems and processes. If you have some already documented, get the new starter to check them. If you do not have anything in place, now is the ideal time to get the new starter to document everything they see as part of their induction. Not only do they learn what they need to know, but you also get your systems documented. This is a massive win-win!

Step 13: Team Meetings

I am not a fan of meetings for the sake of meetings. Yet, to guarantee everyone stays on the *"same page,"* communication with your teams in a meeting is essential. Time and time again, *"lack of communication"* appears high on the list of *"reasons for leaving"* in exit interviews. The ratio I mentioned in Time Mastery still stands true here. For every one-minute we spend being proactive, we will save 10 minutes having to be reactive. When you first start having these meetings, they might take longer than expected. The more meetings you have, and the more regularly you have them, the less time they will take.

An important area to get right before starting these meetings is the Agenda, and of equal importance are the timings for the Agenda items. If you are not careful, these meetings can end up lasting all day. Not only does this waste your time, but it also sets a depressing tone for future meetings. Before you know it, people are dreading these meetings and do not come to them with the right attitude, rendering them ineffective.

I also like to ensure that any actions are captured and assigned. There are few worse things than actions not being completed. It sets a dangerous culture in motion around accountability. Every meeting should start with the actions from the previous meeting. If the individual assigned actions during the last meeting has not done them, they explain why. I'm not talking about bullying or a toxic culture. I'm just talking about healthy adult to adult accountability.

You need to agree the meeting rules, especially around mindset and above/below the line. You want to avoid people just coming to moan and finger point. This behaviour will drain the life out of the proceedings. Yes, if people have issues, you want them aired, but once they have got things off their chests, you need them also to suggest possible solutions. Your values would be a great starting point to ensure things proceed properly.

I like asking other people in the team to Chair the meetings. I have seen it work well. Post a schedule where everyone gets a chance to Chair the meeting. Members of the team alternating as meeting Chair serves as an opportunity to see who wants to progress to management positions. Also, different people chairing the meetings brings something different to the proceedings.

You need someone to take minutes and to document everything, especially the actions. Get the minutes and actions circulated to everyone no later than 24 hours after the meeting has concluded.

There are different sorts of team meetings.

- **General Team Meetings.** The frequency of these depends on the size of your business and team. A happy middle ground that satisfies most businesses is to have this kind of meeting every fortnight. The agenda here is typically dominated by "IN" the business matters.
- **Directors / Management Meetings.** The frequency here can be monthly. Here you discuss more "ON" the business matters like the plan and higher-level strategy.

Here you should also discuss finances. Discuss where you are versus forecast etc.

- **Sales & Marketing Meetings.** These must happen every week. Here you will go through your pipelines and discuss prospects and where they are in the pipeline. Also, review marketing strategies.

- **Quarterly Team Meetings.** The frequency of these is given in the title, but some clients do these bi-annually or annually. Here, you will prepare a presentation and give everyone an update on where we are as a business and what the plans are going forwards. Convene these meetings off-site, and they should have a fun/social aspect to them too. For example, go paintballing afterward.

As the leader, like the 1-2-1's, you need to get used to holding briefings regularly. These meetings become your platform to ensure smooth and consistent communication. The real trick again is consistency. You must ensure that the rhythm of these meetings is maintained. As soon as you stop doing them, you will notice things do not run as smoothly as before. Do not stop doing them!

Step 14: Common Goal

I have spoken in Destination Mastery about the importance of goal setting, but here, I want to go one step further and explain why it's so important to share goals with the team.

You may have heard a story about a Management Consultant who was desperate to work with McLaren Formula 1 team many years ago. He was continually rebuffed by the Executive Team at McLaren when he tried to get his foot in the door with them. He persisted, and finally, they agreed to his request for a meeting. Realising that he would only have one shot at this to convince the team that they needed his help, he thought of one thing he would use in his meeting. He thought of the common goal. He knew that 98% of businesses say that all their team is aware of the goals. But in reality, no one is. He realised that this would be his *"in."*

On the morning of the meeting, the Management Consultant arrived at the McLaren Formula 1 HQ in Woking, Surrey. The Management Consultant saw a gentleman in McLaren overalls sweeping leaves in the car park. Not to miss an opportunity to have even more ammunition for his meeting with the top brass, the Consultant approached the McLaren employee. When they made eye contact, the Consultant asked, *"Excuse me, can I ask what you are doing?"* Without hesitation, the gentleman sweeping the leaves replied, *"I am helping Lewis Hamilton become Formula 1 World Champion."* It is fair to say that the Consultant never expected that reply!

When you switch on a torch, the light dissipates. But with a focus, that same light can cut through metal. When everyone aligns themselves with one common goal, the same thing happens. Can you imagine the energy that would flow through your business when every single person was enrolled and inspired by one common goal? The common goal should be an annual objective. This annual objective is different from the vision, which, in theory, is never achieved.

Many business owners tell me that they are worried about their team's reaction to any financial goal, especially if the business achieves the goal. They do not want the team thinking that they are *"rolling in it"* because then the inevitable requests for a pay rise will come in like a flood. As said before, if any of your team have an issue with you making money for all the effort and sacrifice you put in, then they should not be in your team. Yet, you already should have a fair system for awarding pay raises and bonuses in place, so, you should not worry about what your team might or might not say.

So, as the leader, think of the common goal. Make it exciting. Make hitting it a win-win for all parties. Talk about it all the time; update people where the business is against the goal every day, week, or month. If you hit it, have a party to celebrate!

Step 15: Training and Development Plans

Opportunities to develop and their relationship with their Line Manager are the main reasons why an individual will stay in a role. It is your job not just to pay lip service to training and development but do something about it too. You can attract the best talent if you become a business that is serious about developing your people. Business owners lament that they invest significant sums of time and money in an individual, only for them to leave shortly after. I remind them that the average time an employee now stays in a role is approximately three years. The time of employment in each position varies depending on which research you use. Typically, the older they are, the longer they tend to stay in a role. So, in those three years, if you invested in that person, and they systemised the role and left the business better than when they joined it, what is the issue?

Training and development should be a section in the 1-2-1. You must put the onus on the individuals to come to you and tell you about where they want to improve. The business should also suggest potential career paths for the individual. You do not need this to be a fancy document. You can get by with a simple conversation and then some simple steps the individual will take. Please document all these conversations as you might need them to performance manage someone later down the line.

Online learning has taken massive leaps in recent years, and your team members can consume the training sitting at a desk with a laptop. There is no reason why everyone cannot learn and develop in any area they wish.

Every business should have a training budget and should set aside time for training and development. A few of my clients set the gold standard here as far as I am concerned. They give all Friday afternoon up for training and development. Can you imagine what message that sends to your people about how much you value them? Some even go as far as letting people learn things that have nothing to do with their business. For example, one client let one of their team members learn knitting!

Remember, if your business is a direct reflection of your people, surely it makes sense for them to grow. If they do, so will the business. Please be the type of business where you look after your people and invest in them to become the best versions of themselves. It will pay you back.

Step 16: Succession Planning

At all times and all levels of the business structure, there should be the next generation of team members ready to step-up. If anyone leaves, there should already be a ready-made successor in the existing team. You protect the business through this succession planning. During the 1-2-1, use the current and future Organisational Charts to discuss that individual's desired career path. The plan should always have a replacement in mind should the incumbent leave. Do you see how all of the 16 steps I mention in this chapter are essential?

In Zappos, they insist that everyone joining the business must spend their first few weeks learning every department. At the last count, 87% of the people who join, stay with Zappos. When a vacancy occurs, they promote from within the organisation. Then they bring someone else new in right at the bottom to work their way up. Zappos has a great culture and one that will serve a business well.

A mistake made often is where the best person doing a job gets promoted to management. The best salesperson, for example, does not necessarily make the best sales manager. Doing this could create a *"double whammy"* of losing your best salesperson's sales as well as lessening your sales team's overall performance because it now had a poor manager. All because you promoted the best salesperson to the sales manager when they were not the right person for that job. The best football managers, with a few notable exceptions, were not the best players. The team members will need training, mentoring, and coaching to become good managers. Do not expect them to manage well because they were good at the job.

Give people regular time with other people to start to become more familiar with the next step up in the Organisational Chart. When someone does leave, you will have a natural successor. This can only be a good thing for the business.

CHAPTER 15

TEAM SUMMARY

As I said before, your people will make your lives relatively easy or very hard. The one it is for you will depend on you. Give your people the time and energy they deserve. Just because some people have let you down in the past and no doubt will do in the future, that is no reason to think that everyone will be like that.

The most critical word in management is consistency. With the 16-steps, you now have a system to ensure you can manage your people effectively and, more importantly, consistently.

CHAPTER 16

FREEDOM

So, now you have a business that is working without you. Systems are running the business, people are running the systems, and you, or your successor is leading the people. Please do not fall into the trap of thinking your work or the work of your successors is complete. Embrace the principles of *"constant and never-ending improvement"* and *"we are growing, or we are dying."* You must continue to work on the Cycle of Business Success. The foundations you laid at Mastery might not be solid enough to support the size of business you are now. Go back and revisit them. I hope you will continuously review the sections and make improvements as you go along. That's why the model I have shared with you is a cycle, it never ends. Remember, never stop working ON the business.

There is a phrase you may have heard before – *"get out of your way."* For some people reading this book, they already have a business that works without them. For the others, I hope that by implementing what you have read in this book, you will also end up there. Unfortunately, most people in the position to step away from their business will not do so because of their mindset. Early on in this book, I said that mindset drives 100% of what we do. There could not be a better example than business owners that reached the Freedom stage, but told themselves that they could not possibly be away from the business. It would all collapse without them.

You need to look inwardly to understand what the fear is of stepping away. What are your belief systems telling you? Are they saying that it will all go wrong if you dare to take some time away? If you believe this, you will never leave the business to do what you want to for yourself. There will be fear. Fear is natural and understandable. Remember, FEAR stands for False Expectations Appearing Real. For those of us who are parents, you will remember what you were like when you left your baby with someone else for the first time. You felt mortified that something terrible would happen while you tried to enjoy your first adult date night since your child was born. Usually, this resulted in you leaving the restaurant after the starters and rushing back to relieve the babysitter. Your business is like a child to you. You gave birth to it. You have nurtured it, seen it grow and prosper. You have been frustrated by it, stressed by it, but you are also proud of it. Like our children, we will sooner or later have to let it spread its wings and fly itself. Leaving your children for the first time is scary, but it is part of the evolutionary process for a parent, and it is the same for a business owner.

If you have built your business so that systems run the business, people run the systems, then all you now need to do is recruit a General Manager/MD/CEO to lead the people. You can come in once a week

Freedom

or monthly for the board meeting and assume your position as Chairman to oversee proceedings. The new person will run the system you created. They will present the P&L, Dashboard, Cashflow, Marketing plan, Sales numbers, and they will show where you are against the 12-month goals. You have all the controls in place to ensure that things are on track. If you need to, you can suggest the necessary course corrections.

You now have the job to act as a sounding board, Coach, Mentor, for your replacement. You must let go and give the replacement time and space to run things. They will have their KPI's, and you do their 1-2-1 with them every month to ensure they remain on track. This way, you are delegating, not abdicating. You built this system. Trust yourself that you did a good job and stand back.

The challenge you face now is what to do with this newfound free time? Do you do some of the things that are on your Dream Chart? Do you spend more time with family and friends? Do you dedicate some time to volunteering for your favourite causes? What about that hobby you always wanted to develop but never had the time? Whatever it is, put it in your diary. Remember the *"law of vacuum?"* If you do not put things in your diary, nature will fill it for you with unimportant and unfulfilling *"stuff."* The other reason to find something to do is that you need to keep your mind active. I have heard many stories of people who retire from their jobs or sell their businesses, and within 12 months, they are sadly dead. If the mind is not needed for anything, the body thinks the same and starts to shut down. Someone has worked all their adult lives, and now they have time for themselves; sadly, however, their body decides to either shut down or rob them of their health. They cannot do the things they had dreamt of doing. What a travesty! Do not let this happen to you. Please keep your mind active. Keep growing.

What about taking these learnings and applying them to another business? After all, every business on earth follows the same principles. At the time of writing, I have the Business Coaching business, an online business selling baby products, and a property investment business. These are different businesses, but I apply the same principles to them all. You can do this too because you have a business education for life now. Does the prospect of owning many businesses with MD's in all of them excite you? If it does, then go and do it. Follow the same process I have outlined in this book, and it will work for you.

The world needs entrepreneurs. Entrepreneurs create jobs, give people opportunities, and create abundance. Go and make a difference in this world!

SUMMARY

Our vision is to give every business owner a business to be proud of and a life worth living. By reading this book, you have everything needed to move you and your business towards that vision. If it does, then writing this book will all have been worthwhile.

Nothing will happen if you do not take action however. You can either say that the world is against you, or you can ask, *"So, what am I going to do about it?"* Remember, the only thing we can control is our response to events.

Some of you might still be struggling with the *"how?"* I have outlined the tactics and the tools to use. If you need more help to put in place the things I have talked about, please get in touch. Check out our website at www.reachbusinesscoaching.co.uk.

If you want to chat, drop me a line at admin@reachbusinesscoaching.co.uk. I would love to know what you thought about the book and if you have implemented any of the strategies. I am excited to know what the result has been.

Please also connect with us on social media:

- **Facebook** – REACHBusinessCoaching
- **Instagram** – reachcoachinguk

- **Twitter** – REACHCoachingUK
- **YouTube** – REACH Business Coaching
- **LinkedIn** – jasdarar

I also invite you to join my online coaching programme as an excellent way to get some cost-effective support to implement the strategies you have read in this book, and so much more. The programme will give you every single bit of detailed support and handholding you would need to build your business. Regardless of where you are in the world, and what type and size of business you have, this online coaching programme has everything you need. I have separated the online programme into fortnightly modules with easy to understand *"how-to"* videos and templates. The templates are of the documents discussed in this book, and lots more. Finally, you get access to our exclusive members only Facebook group. The Facebook group will give you all the ongoing support and encouragement you need. Find out more about this incredible programme at www.reachclub.co.uk.

I have given you as much as I possibly could in this book. I hope, with all of my being, that you have got value from it. Please take action and begin the process of giving yourself a business to be proud of, and a life worth living.

Thank you.